CAPITAL ACCUMULATION AND ECONOMIC DEVELOPMENT

CAPITAL ACCUMULATION AND ECONOMIC DEVELOPMENT

Edited with Introductions by
SHANTI S. TANGRI
H. PETER GRAY
WAYNE STATE UNIVERSITY

D. C. HEATH AND COMPANY · BOSTON

Library of Congress Catalog Card Number: 67-16806

PRINTED JUNE 1967

CONTENTS

III. STRATEGIES OF CAPITAL ACCUMULATION

IV. THE ALLOCATION OF CAPITAL

INTRODUCTION

Neither the importance nor the complexity of economic development needs emphasis: both are great. The complexity of the development process may be said to hinge upon the need for a fundamental change in the economic and social processes taking place in a nation in the course of development.[1] Because of its many dimensions, economic development is best approached, at least at first, by studying one component of the process in greater detail than the other, equally important, components. This volume is devoted to the study of the role of capital accumulation in the development process, the limitations of capital accumulation as a single remedy for economic backwardness, and the problem involved in assuring that capital is indeed accumulated and used to its best advantage.

Since one of the great disparities observable in any comparison of rich and poor nations is the amount of capital available per head of population or per unit of labor, a *prima facie* case exists for the necessity of capital accumulation to the process of economic development. However, capital accumulation cannot by itself be relied upon to achieve economic development nor is it inevitable that resources will be freed for the formation of capital or that any resources not used for consumption will be used for capital formation.

Traditionally, to economists the term capital has meant factories, machine tools, buildings and other types of reproducible productive equipment. In studies of economic development, the importance of other types of inputs to the process of production, almost taken for granted in richer nations, has required economists to broaden the scope of their concept of capital. Plant, equipment and inventories in industry and agriculture need little explanation: they comprise the traditional concept.[2] Social overhead capital consists of transport facilities, communications networks, public utilities, buildings of government and the equipment necessary for the provision of public services and the maintenance of social overhead

[1] *Economic Development,* edited by Laura Randall, in this series addresses itself to the problem of the influence of the political framework on the development process.

[2] Traditional concepts also include housing.

capital. This type of capital is necessary for the efficient operation of the economy but is assumed to play no direct role in the productive process. Finally, the acquired skills of the population — human capital — are recognized as being productive in themselves and as necessary for the full utilization of up-to-date plant and equipment and modern technology.

Once the definition of capital has been broadened beyond its traditional limits, two difficulties arise. The first difficulty lies in delimiting the scope of the concept. Should technological improvements be regarded as capital accumulation? If so, should the improvements be measured only as they are incorporated into the capital stock or as the improvements become available for use? It is tempting to conceive of capital as such an all-embracing factor of production that all economic growth which is not directly attributable to other factors may be accounted for by capital accumulation. But such a definition can lead to paradoxical situations such as the stock of capital being expanded (diminished) on paper by a political decree which increases (diminishes) social and economic efficiency.

The best definition for general purposes is, perhaps, one which includes only plant and equipment, social overhead and human capital. Then capital accumulation may be limited to the process by which a net acquisition of future resources is achieved only at the expense of foregoing current consumption.[3]

The second difficulty is the question of dividing newly-acquired capital among the three subcategories, *i.e.*, the problem of the optimum allocation of a given amount of capital. This difficulty is subsumed in aggregate models of an economy by the simple assumption that the work force will, when fully employed, exactly meet the needs of the existing capital stock both in quantity *and* quality and that social overhead capital is adequate to service the product of the stock of plant and equipment.

The rate at which capital is accumulated and the rate at which the newly acquired capital will stimulate growth can be shown quite simply by a graphic presentation of the Harrod-Domar model.[4] This model is the most famous of the aggregate models of economic growth, but must be used with caution. While it provides a revealing mechanism of the contribution of capital to the growth of income, its assumptions are numerous and varied.

The Harrod-Domar economy is one of permanent full employment which has no international trading relations nor any government sector. The volume of investment in any period is net investment; it represents

[3] The measurement of capital presents many difficulties but the usual method is to assess its worth in terms of the foregone consumption.

[4] This model was originally developed in R. F. Harrod, "An Essay in Dynamic Theory," *Economic Journal* (March 1939), pp. 14–33: and, Evsey Domar, "Expansion and Employment," *American Economic Review,* XXXVII (March 1947); see also R. F. Harrod, *Towards a Dynamic Economics* (London, 1948). The authors have elaborated on this model in subsequent publications.

a net addition to the capital stock of the country, and the capital depreciated in the course of production has been replaced. The new capital, formed by the saving in one period, comes into production at the beginning of the following period. No distinction is made among the types of capital acquired. No technological advance is posited. Finally, the labor force is assumed to grow at the rate necessary to service the net increase in the capital stock.

A DIAGRAMMATIC MODEL OF ECONOMIC GROWTH

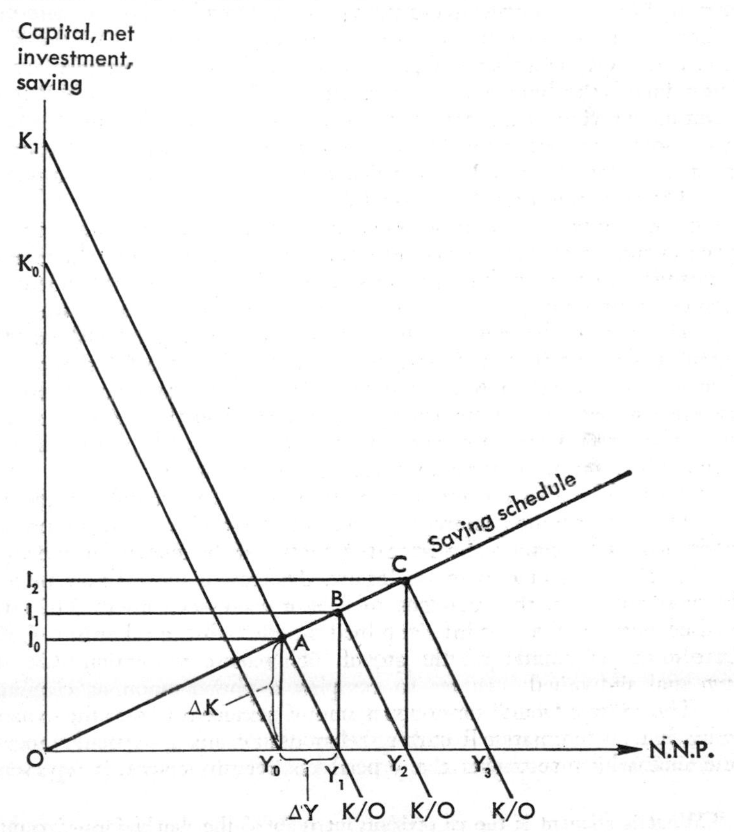

NOTE: The K/O ratio, OK_0/OY_0, is drawn as downward-sloping because it simplifies the graph. The ratio is, of course, positive, not negative as the slope of the line implies. The assumption of a constant K/O ratio means that the incremental capital output ratios ($\Delta K/\Delta Y$, or the ICOR's) in all periods are equal to the average capital output ratios, *i.e.*, $OK_0/OY_0 = Y_0A/Y_0Y_1 = Y_1B/Y_1Y_2$ etc.

In Figure 1 net national product is measured along the horizontal axis; saving, net investment and capital are measured along the vertical axis. The saving schedule shows the relation between income and saving (consumption foregone): it is drawn so that the marginal propensity is equal to the average propensity to save. Point A shows the equilibrium level of saving and investment (I_0O) and the N.N.P. (OY_0) produced with capital stock OK_0 in year 0. As a result of the net investment I_0 in year 0, the capital stock has been increased by that amount and this capital becomes productive in year 1. N.N.P. in year 1 will be higher than in year 0 by the product of the new capital. How big this increase will be depends upon the capital/output ratio (K/O in Figure 1):[5] the K/O ratio (OK_0/OY_0) in this model is assumed to be a constant relationship determined by technological factors. In year 1, the higher N.N.P. generates more saving, and therefore more net investment (BY_1) must, under the assumptions of the model, be forthcoming. The greater addition to the capital stock in year 1 means that the absolute increase in output in year 2 exceeds the increase in output in year 1.

The beauty of this model is its simplicity. It assumes the economy to be operating on its production-possibility curve and then shows how the generation of new capital (reinforced by the necessary increments to the labor supply) will shift the curve outward by ever-increasing amounts. The magnitude of the shift will depend upon two relationships: the saving schedule and the capital/output ratio. The greater the rate of saving, the greater the rate of investment in any one period and therefore the greater the rate of growth of N.N.P. The lower the K/O ratio (*i.e.*, the higher the product of each new piece of capital), the greater the rate of growth from any given rate of capital accumulation.

This model allows for continuous growth and, presumably therefore, for development to be achieved by a steady progression. In this sense the model differs fundamentally from the theory of "take-off" developed by W. W. Rostow.[6] According to Rostow, the growth process may be subdivided into five, distinct stages: (1) the traditional society; (2) the establishment of the preconditions for take-off; (3) the take-off; (4) the drive to maturity and, (5) the age of high mass consumption. Clearly, any analysis which separates so complex a phenomenon as economic growth into "watertight" compartments must achieve clarity at the expense of realism. Nonetheless, Rostow's theory has provided a useful frame of reference which spotlights the crucial changes in emphasis in society

[5] What is relevant is the capital/output ratio of the newly formed capital. However, this ratio is assumed to be equal to the K/O ratio of the general stock of capital.

[6] See "The Take-Off into Self-Sustained Growth," *Economic Journal,* LXVI (March 1956), pp. 25–48; and *The Stages of Economic Growth* (Cambridge, 1960); for some critical evaluations of this thesis see the contributions of Simon Kuzets and Robert Solow in *The Economics of Take-Off,* ed. W. W. Rostow.

which must take place in the process of economic development. The traditional society is characterized by a pre-Newtonian culture, static per capita output at a low level, primitive technology, and social values concerned with stability and the preservation of the *status quo* rather than with change and innovation. The establishment of the preconditions for take-off is a period of gradual change — lasting perhaps a century or more — during which questioning attitudes, human skills, entrepreneurial aptitudes, and some physical capital are acquired together with the growth of rationality which promotes the search for achieving ends by the most efficient means. The crucial stage of development is a period of very heavy capital formation of a generation or more. This third stage, the period of take-off, is for our purposes the most important; it is initiated by a sharp stimulus, such as a political revolution.[7] During take-off, there is a positive, sustained, and self-reinforcing response to the stimulus, an ongoing change in the production processes, a rising per capita income, and a rise in the "proportion of net investment" to national income, from, say, 5% to over 10%, definitely outstripping the likely population pressure.[8]

The main elements of Rostow's thesis may be explained in terms of Figure 1. During the second stage, the development of the nation has proceeded slowly in accordance with the model. Social overhead and human capital are laboriously acquired. These forms of capital have very high capital/output ratios so that the effect of capital formation on income is almost imperceptible from year to year. As people tend to consume most of their income, the pre-take-off society can be seen as having a very flat savings schedule and a very steep capital/output schedule. Then, in response to some major stimulus, the proportion of capital devoted to overhead and human capital decreases and the proportion devoted to directly productive capital grows more quickly. A shift in the investment pattern has occurred. The directly productive capital enjoys a much lower capital/output ratio so that the change in investment pattern makes the incremental capital/output ratio schedule much flatter. In addition, the large profits gained by new productive enterprises redistribute income within the society toward the new class of business men. Since these entrepreneurs tend to be thrifty, the redistribution of income reinforced by the development of an efficient system of financial intermediaries causes the savings schedule to shift upward. Thus, in terms of Figure 1, the take-off may be said to enhance the rate of growth by generating permanent and sizeable shifts in the two crucial components of the Harrod-Domar model, the savings rate and the capital output ratio.

[7] Rostow, *Stages; op. cit.*, pp. 36–37.

[8] Rostow, pp. 37–38, 46–50, 52–53, 57; Rostow assumes a capital output ratio of between 3 and 3.5. This implies, therefore, that population grows under 3% per year during the take-off period. For an elaboration of this point see Myint and Tangri in Section II of this volume.

Capital formation is necessary for economic development but it is not a panacea for poverty, and its contribution to the growth process can be easily overemphasized. With the exception of the selection "Capital Accumulation: The Core Process," the selections in the first section of this volume are arguments against what we may call "the univariate hypothesis" — that capital accumulation alone is the key to economic development. The pieces by Hans W. Singer and John Kenneth Galbraith emphasize the need for consideration of the noneconomic factors in any analysis of the process of development. A. K. Cairncross and Shanti S. Tangri each criticize the univariate hypothesis on economic grounds, Cairncross questioning the causality, and Tangri the automaticity, of investment, both of which are inherent in the univariate hypothesis.

Galbraith puts the role of capital in perspective, thus setting the stage for the discussion in Section II. If capital is indeed necessary for the economic development of the underdeveloped countries, how much capital is required and where could it be obtained? Myint questions the capital output ratios and the assumptions underlying such computations. Despite such disagreements, there is a general agreement among economists that the volume of capital needed is such as to require substantially increased rates of internal saving and capital inflows from abroad. Finally, Tangri outlines the general case for increased internal saving.

Prebisch discusses the role of regional and international cooperation in this context while Ellis outlines the stake of the United States in providing foreign aid to supplement the internal efforts for generating savings for development.

In addition to being indispensible to the basic process of development, capital accumulation plays another important role in the modern world. For altruistic or political motives, richer nations are currently concerned with aiding poorer countries in their development plans. Aid, in the form of capital, can be transferred internationally without drastic interference in the internal affairs of the recipient nations. By making hard currency or credits available to poorer nations, the rate of capital accumulation can be increased. Alternative forms of developmental assistance may be more tenuous in their contribution to development and therefore more difficult to justify to taxpayers in the donor nation and to nationalists in the recipient country.

Whether capital requirements are large or small, it is important to know the optimal strategy for capital accumulation and the optimal allocation of the available capital among various uses. The smaller the supplies of capital in relation to requirements, the more urgent the need to answer these questions which are the concern of the contributors in the last two sections of readings.

In Part Three Nurkse argues that the smallness of the market inhibits the inducement to invest, thereby keeping the productivity of labor low. This in turn keeps incomes low and the market small. The remedy, Nurkse suggests, is "balanced growth," or an attack on a wide front of poverty which expands productivity and incomes in various industries which will create wide markets for the goods produced. Hagen attacks the notion that vicious circles such as postulated by Nurkse are the real culprits preventing economic growth. Ellis, while in agreement with the need for a growth process in which demands and supplies of various outputs are in balance, takes issue with the theories of "Big Push" derived from the notion of vicious circles. Myint analyzes the interrelationships between these two theoretical progenies of vicious circles. Hirschman's espousal of unbalanced growth and the contending arguments for balanced growth lead Singer to an attempt at synthesis.

In Part Four, Leibenstein outlines the disagreements among economists on problems of policy in this area. The U. N. article discusses the relative importance of allocating resources between the physical infrastructure and directly productive activities. Myint examines the appropriate policy for investing in the social infrastructure. Finally, Schultz makes the case for education as an investment in human skills and abilities.

PART ONE

THE CONCEPT AND THE ROLE OF CAPITAL

INTRODUCTION

Ever since Adam Smith equated saving and investment with private and public virtue economists, historians, sociologists, political scientists and others interested in social change have continued to focus on capital accumulation as the key variable in economic development. Conservative bankers, capitalists and farmers, and revolutionary Marxists share this "puritanic" belief. Hans W. Singer discusses "the evolution of thought" from the classical "puritan" model to the Keynesian model of the interwar years and the human investment model of postwar years.

The "puritan" model emphasized the curbing of appetites to facilitate savings and investment as central to the process of developing a capital-poor economy. The Keynesian model, born in the context of idle men and machines postulated the complementarity rather than the competitiveness of consumption and investment, or, as Singer puts it, "the best way of making sure of having jam tomorrow is to have jam today." The human investment model, while combining "the necessary emphasis in model I on the importance of capital accumulation with the emphasis in model II on the need to increase consumption . . . has great weaknesses . . . it treats human welfare as an instrument . . . and the increase of GNP or the accumulation of physical capital as a final value." Singer argues that the stage is now set for the development of a fourth model for understanding as well as promoting economic growth as an integral part of the process of social development.

Shanti S. Tangri argues that the dichotomy of consumption and investment underlying most models of development is somewhat misleading because consumption has productivity effects; the increased productivity resulting from more capital may be partly offset by the decreased productivity resulting from decreased consumption, and therefore what is good for growth is some optimum level of consumption and not minimum consumption. He also makes a case for broader and more consistent definitions of investment in men and machines, physical structures and social institutions. Indeed investment, or creation of productive resources, interpreted and measured conventionally—as is done by the United Nations—accounts for only a small part of the spectacular growth of output in the developed societies. This conclusion of A. K. Cairncross for the British economy has been supported by various studies of the U.S. economy and has stimulated the search for alternative sources of growth in various forms of technical change or in education (model III in the manner of Singer).[1]

Galbraith reviews the controversy about the relative importance of capital, technical knowledge, trained manpower, planning and the social and political ingredients of economic growth and reasons that in the earlier stages of development investment in administration, education, health and political reforms is more important while in the later stages investment in machines and technology becomes more important: "At each stage of this continuum [extending from the tribal to the most developed societies] there is an appropriate policy for further advance. What is appropriate at one stage is wrong at another."

[1] Much of this growing literature is highly technical. A few of the important contributions include:

Moses Abramovitz, *Resources and Output Trends in the United States Since 1870,* National Bureau of Economic Research, Occasional Paper 52, New York, 1956 (also in the *American Economic Review,* May 1956, pp. 5–23); Robert M. Solow, "Technical Change and the Aggregate Production Function," *Review of Economics and Statistics,* August 1957, pp. 312–20; and Edward F. Denison, *The Sources of Economic Growth in the United States,* Committee for Economic Development, Washington, 1962.

HANS W. SINGER

Social Development: Key Growth Sector*

THE VIEWS of economists in this matter [of development] have performed a sort of cycle in the last 20 years or so. About 20 years ago when the attention of economists had not yet been attracted to the then very peripheral problems of underdeveloped countries, they tended to believe that these were matters of interest mainly to sociologists, anthropologists, psychologists or other lesser breed of this kind.

Then economic development became the big growth sector in the economic science. In the flush of enthusiasm, economists tended to think in terms of economic growth models. Those were the great days of the Harrod-Domar formula, of average and incremental capital-output ratios, of rates of saving and investment, of closing and widening gaps in gross national product (GNP). But then came the days of disillusionment. Doubts began to creep in whether the matter was as simple as that. What was the meaning of GNP gaps when the GNP concept was applied to countries with subsistence economies, with tribal or other communal forms of organization, with different economic motivations? What was the meaning of capital formation or saving in such conditions?

The doubts were reinforced when quantitative research arrived at the conclusion that capital investment failed to account for much or most of economic growth, that there was a large unexplained "residue." It was found that when you deal with unhealthy, undernourished, illiterate people, some extra food or the eradication of malaria or some instruction or training can be more important in raising their productivity than physical capital; what then becomes of the conventional line of division between consumption and investment? The ICOR's of the Harrod-Domar formula turned out to be so unstable as to be useless as an instrument of economic planning

* Reprinted by permission of the Society for International Development, from "Social Development: Key Growth Sector" *International Development Review* by Hans W. Singer, Vol. VII, No. 1, March 1965, pp. 3–5.

according to a purely economic model, even though it took economists many years to draw this obvious conclusion.

Even worse, the social worm was right inside the core of the economic apple: The rate of investment turned out to be determined by investment opportunities, but the perception of such opportunities was a matter of the quality of people and involved pre-investment work; moreover, the utilization of such investment opportunities as were perceived, were found to be a matter of the motivation of people, the right kind of communication with them and of a social structure which permitted people to utilize such opportunities.

Thus wherever he turned, the development economist, as he began to turn away from his textbooks and learned about underdeveloped countries, was driven back towards the earlier position, viz. that those queer fish and lesser breeds – sociologists, anthropologists, psychologists, etc. – had after all a lot to contribute to the problems of economic development. So we were back to the earlier position, but with this important difference: the economists no longer said: "This subject does not interest us; it can be left to the sociologists, etc." This time they said: "The social aspects of development are too important to be neglected by us and left to the sociologists. The problem interests us too much to leave it to them. We must move in and find a broader basis for an understanding of the problems and approaches to policy." It is thus that the social aspects of development have become for the economists a growth sector within the general growth sector of economic development. We have, therefore, here the very thing which every stock-exchange investor or broker is looking for – a growth sector within a growth sector.

During the last 20 years, therefore, the wheel has come full circle but we are not back where we were before. We are further forward, and we are at a new point of departure from which a new journey can begin. This is the road ahead which the Dutch Government perceived, and for which with far-sighted generosity they provided the vehicle. This is the journey on which the new UN Research Institute for Social Development is now setting out.

DIFFERENT MODELS OF ECONOMIC AND SOCIAL GROWTH

The evolution of thought which has been briefly described above can be expressed more precisely and purposefully by a succession of models characteristic of the different modes of approach. We may start off with Model I which we may call the classical puritan model of growth. In this model consumption is reduced, the saving is invested in productive capital, the productive capital produces both more productive capital and more consumption goods so that ultimately the cut in consumption can be restored. In this model, as will be seen, at any given time economic growth requires a cut in consumption — that is why I call this model "puritan" — although in the end result an increase in consumption may result. It is a case of jam yesterday and jam the day after tomorrow, but no jam today or even tomorrow. The cut in consumption is an instrumental variable, the resulting capital formation is the target or objective, although a final increase in consumption is dimly on the horizon. However, in the strictly classical model even this dim vision of jam the day after tomorrow is destroyed by Malthusian increase in numbers, or by increasing inequality of income distribution owing to the fixed quantity of land, etc.

Next came the Keynesian Model II, distinctly less puritan. Under this model, consumption and capital formation grow and decline together, tied together by the multiplier and the accelerator. Provided that there are latent or unemployed resources in the economy, the best way of making sure of having jam tomorrow is to have jam today. *You can eat your cake and have it — in fact you must eat your cake if you want to have it.* This Keynesian model obviously is of great interest to students of underdeveloped countries. The analogy is striking. Just as in underdeveloped countries underconsumption weakens people, stops them from being fully productive and sets up vicious circles of low productivity — low output — poverty — no savings — continued poverty — continued undernourishment, etc., *ad infinitum,* so in the Keynesian Model II under-employment gnaws at the vitals of the economy, and sets up vicious circles of depression — unemployment — lack of investment — loss of output — more unemployment — more depression, etc., *ad infinitum.*

All the same, in spite of similarities, the Keynesian Model II cannot serve as a model of social development in underdeveloped countries. It should be remembered that it is based on the assumption of latent and unemployed resources — or on elastic supply functions, in more technical language. This, however, is not the condition of underdeveloped countries. They are characterized by inelastic supplies, by all-pervading scarcity of resources — or so it would seem at least on a first approach. You certainly cannot start off by stimulating consumption, for where are the resources? There simply is no jam today with which you can start. Now, does it follow from this that we are driven back to the harsh puritan classical Model I? It does not follow. For, although the scarcity of resources may be identical to Model I and the model we are seeking for the underdeveloped countries, the remedy is not. The remedy in Model I, let us remember, was to cut consumption. But the implicit assumption was that you can do this without reducing productivity. But in underdeveloped countries you deal with people whose productivity is already undermined by insufficient consumption. To cut consumption will make matters worse.

So, we are next presented with a new Model III which I would call the "human investment model." This model is based on the basic notion of "human capital" and its role in the development process. It has obviously some attractive features: it combines the necessary emphasis in Model I on the importance of capital accumulation, with the emphasis in Model II on the need to increase consumption. But it has also great weaknesses: above all it treats human welfare as an instrument, while it treats the increase of GNP or the accumulation of physical capital as a final value. Thus, the apparent beautiful simplicity of Model III in combining the useful elements for underdeveloped countries from the two previous models is bought at the high price of inverting, or perverting the true relationship between human welfare and national income or physical capital.

There is something, not only degrading, but also misleading and leading to wrong policy approaches, in the notion of "human investment" or "human capital." The misleading nature of this approach lies in the fact that any improvement in human welfare which leads to an increase in income or capital will be called "productive investment," while any increase in human welfare which does not do this will be called "consumption." But this is obviously unreal: the whole purpose of the former "productive" type of increase is also that it should lead in its turn to increased consumption or welfare. Hence on policy grounds there is no general case for a priority of the "productive" expenditures which lead *indirectly,* i.e., via higher incomes and increased resources, to higher levels of living, as compared with other expenditures, labelled "consumptive," which do so *directly* without a detour through higher incomes. Moreover, by establishing this sharp dichotomy between these two types – "human investment" on the one hand, and "consumptive welfare" on the other hand – Model III deprives policy makers of the common standards or measurements by which to allocate total resources amongst these different purposes.

THE ELEMENTS OF MODEL IV

Thus, while gratefully accepting Model III as a useful stepping stone on our journey, it is not what we really need and want. Or rather, it is only an ingredient of the Model IV which we need. We can say something about the main features of Model IV, if it is to be relevant to the underdeveloped countries of today. We may take our clue from the basic thesis that "the problem of the underdeveloped countries is not just growth, but development. Development is growth *plus* change; change, in turn, is social and cultural as well as economic, and qualitative as well as quantitative."[1]

The key concept must be the improved quality of people's life. This is a notion that combines both growth and change. Improvements in the quality of people are at the same time consumption and investment; objective and instruments; demand for resources and supply of resources. Health measures are the instrument for improving the quality of people – but better health is also the desired result and in turn a source of increased productivity which provides the necessary resources for further health expenditures. Better food is the instrument but better nutrition is also the objective. Better education and training is the instrument of change but the better educated man is also the objective. Better housing is the instrument but it is also the objective. The same is true of social security, of improvements in land tenure and other social indicators of levels of living.

And in providing the initial resources for the better health, better education, better nutrition, better housing, greater social security, etc., which are the keys to growth, we must make people aware of the possibilities of improving the quality of life: we must make people aware of the possibilities of better health and find means of communication with them to utilize the existing facilities to improve their health conditions and adapt better health habits; as also with nutrition, education, better housing and all the other factors discussed. Because of this importance of communication, the problems of education and ignorance are particularly important even though in the debate so far they have perhaps been too much singled out at the expense of other factors involved.

This raising of the level of people's life is both the objective of development, and also its instrument. Improvements in people's level of life can be achieved both directly ("social development") or indirectly via income and economic resources ("economic development"). But a rational development policy must be able to look at these two things as a single entity; where they are taken apart for analytical or descriptive purposes, they must be put together again in policy as well as in final analysis.

[1] *The UN Development Decade: Proposals for Action.* U.N. Publication 62.II.B.2, New York, 1962, pp. 2–3.

Thus, our Model IV must include provision for common measurements of improvements in quality of levels of living, according to its main relevant components, whether they are labelled economic or social. It must contain transformation curves of expenditures into improved levels of living, whether by the direct route or the indirect route. It must contain provision for a "feedback process," in which improved levels of living lead to higher productivity and higher productivity in turn leads to higher levels of living. It must incorporate the four types of relevant movement: (1) the direct improvement of levels of living and its value by itself; (2) improvement leading to growth, i.e., the translation of higher levels of living into increased productivity; (3) growth leading to improvement, that is to say, the use of resources for improvement in levels of living, the income elasticity of various components in levels of living; and (4) growth by itself, the predominant concern of economists in the early phase as represented by the Harrod-Domar model which may now be seen to take its place as one element — but *only* one element — of what we are seeking.

SHANTI S. TANGRI

Investment and Economic Development*

HARD work and habits of savings do not insure economic growth. Peasants in many societies are very hard-working indeed. And many societies save a fair proportion of their output. The crucial difference between economically growing and stagnant societies lies more in the *use* than in the *volume* of savings. Unless savings are put into productive investment, hard work and thrift will produce

* From "Patterns of Investment and Rates of Growth" by Shanti S. Tangri, pp. 14–18. Unpublished Ph.D. dissertation, The University of California, Berkeley, 1961.

hoards of treasure, pyramids, cathedrals, temples, mausoleums, armies, weapons and other symbols of glory, power, beauty or status but not economic growth.

The more the habits of productive investment spread among the population the more readily the supply of savings tends to increase. It is helpful, but not necessary, for the entire or even a major section of the population to become investment-minded. It is necessary, though, that some groups within the community be willing to invest and assume the necessary risks involved in investment and that the community grant them some freedom to maneuver resources into places and combinations where these will be most productive. These groups may be private entrepreneurs, political elites or public servants. The process of economic growth is helped by, and in turn helps, the enhancement of social status and political power of such groups which are pioneering or engineering economic change.

Inefficiency, ineptitude, corruption, miscalculation, carelessness or thoughtlessness in the use of investible resources can lead to serious misallocations and wastages. Thus the will to undertake risks is only one, albeit an important one, of the conditions for successful investment. The will to economize — the will to seize opportunities when and where they exist and to depart from traditional ways of doing things when new ways promise gain, are important ingredients for making investment activity productive and dynamic.

Commonly, when we speak of investment we refer to construction of plants, buildings, machines and inventories. This is done not only because these are the most visible and concrete forms of productive assets, but also because the costs and returns from these are more easily measurable. However, properly speaking, investment refers to all economic activity which involves the use of resources to produce goods and services which produce goods and services. Thus it is as important to use resources for training men to design and operate machines as to build machines. Training of personnel for buying raw materials and labor, borrowing others' savings, keeping accounts and distributing the finished product are as necessary for production as machines or buildings. Thus technical and managerial training and a great deal of education are investments which increase productivity. Similarly, creation of an integrated and supervised credit and capital market is a crucial social investment. It enables existing savings to move into their most productive uses, and stimulates the desire to save and invest among more people. Creation of such markets involves the use of human and other resources for facilitating the roundabout method of production. Viewed this way the

Keynesian aggregates – consumption and investment – as commonly defined and used – are not the most fruitful for purposes of discussing the mechanics of economic growth. It makes much more sense to go back to the classical concepts in which "corn" (or "the wages fund" – symbolizing goods needed to put labor to work), circulating capital, and fixed capital are considered complementary in the production process. To the extent food, clothing, shelter, education and even recreation are provided to enable men to work, these are investments, both for an individual enterprise and for an economy. To the extent these are provided to idle men or exceed the requirement of productivity these are consumption goods. Under this approach measurement is more difficult, but conceptually it is more consistent than the one commonly used by economists and government agencies. In the national income accounting of the United States, an automobile is considered as a consumption or a capital good depending on whether an executive uses it for his official or personal purposes. The rent on the part of his house which he uses for official business is recognized by income tax authorities as a business expense. It would be consistent then, though not convenient perhaps, to consider as investment that part of the consumption of all workers – white or blue collar – which is necessary to aid production. The concept can be refined somewhat. An individual enterprise is less interested in maximizing production than in maximizing net gain. It would thus be interested in its employees' optimum consumption which optimizes production so as to maximize net gain. From the point of view of welfare, an economy may be more interested in that volume of consumption which maximizes total production. For economic growth it appears that this social rather than private "optimum consumption" should be considered an investment. Some of it, like food, is perishable; some, like training and education, is durable. Similarly, the resources spent on the development or improvement of agencies for the making, maintenance, or enforcement of law, and development of markets, goods, and ideas are productive investments.

THE UNITED NATIONS

Capital Accumulation: The Core Process*

THE general rate of development is always limited by shortage of productive factors. If any one scarce factor associated with under-development should be singled out, it would be capital. The final goal of development programming is, therefore, to find the best way of breaking the vicious circle between capital shortage and under-development and to design the most efficient and optimum rate of capital accumulation.

It would be an over-simplification, of course, to regard economic development as a matter of capital accumulation alone. Other things are needed in addition, such as entrepreneurship and training of workers and public administrators. Yet these are seldom possible without some increase in the stock of capital. Therefore capital accumulation may very well be regarded as the core process by which all other aspects of growth are made possible.

Capital increases by investment, and more investment necessitates more savings or foreign assistance. Foreign assistance, if not in the form of grants, means some burden in the future. The extent to which foreign loans can be serviced and repaid will ultimately depend on what can be saved at home in the future. Domestic savings are, therefore, the more reliable source of investment to break the vicious circle of poverty and under-development. But domestic savings can be increased only by a sacrifice in consumption which has to be compared with the future increases in consumption it promises. Investment, moreover, yields different results, depending on the industries in which it is made. In order, therefore, for the government of an under-developed country to design an appropriate plan for development, it must be informed of the quantitative aspects of savings and investment, and their effects on production and consumption.

These quantitative aspects are of crucial importance in determining the most desirable rate of development. It is important, for

* From United Nations, ECAFE, *Programming Techniques for Economic Development* (Bangkok, 1960), pp. 8–13.

one thing, particularly when population is growing rapidly, to estimate the rate of development that would be needed to bring about improvement in *per capita* income or a high rate of employment for the growing work force. Another element which may play a role in estimating a minimum rate of development is the necessity to give a certain minimum size to some projects in order that they are at all economically sound. In some industries where so-called "indivisibilities" play a role, there are such minimum sizes of projects. For the country as a whole, this may mean that only a "big push," as it has been called, can really help to start the process of development. Although this may produce results which appear ambitious in the light of current efforts, it provides a fair indication of the tasks involved in the planning effort.

Whatever the initial approach, there are some useful concepts which should be borne in mind in planning the rate of development. These concepts may conveniently be described in terms of investment. There is, first, the concept of a *minimum rate of investment*, which measures the rate needed to prevent *per capita* income from falling in the face of population growth. A rate of investment somewhat above this minimum is the lowest target at which any plan should aim, even though this may involve a heavy effort when population is growing rapidly. For some countries this may be a rate that can be easily attained on the basis of an effort which does not require any fundamental policy decisions, any changes in attitudes or behaviour patterns, or any improvements in techniques, skills and methods of business or public administration. For these countries, the minimum rate of investment is clearly too low, and is useful only for reference.

A second concept of use in this context is that of a *practical maximum rate of investment*. In theory a maximum rate of investment may refer to a level of capital accumulation which involves saving and investing at least all income above, say, a subsistence level. Clearly, such a maximum is of no practical significance. A practicable maximum may, therefore, be determined differently in the light of the extent to which the population will be willing to accept austerity now, so as to enjoy a higher standard of living in the future. The planner must form his best judgement as to what this practical maximum would be. The rate just defined above is the one to be determined by an evaluation of people's potential propensity to save.

A third concept is that of the highest rate of investment consistent with *absorptive capacity*. Absorptive capacity depends on natural resources, taxes, the labour supply, the level of labour, technical and managerial skills, entrepreneurial capacity, the efficiency of public administration, the extent of "technology-mindedness" of the population, and so on. Such capacity sets a limit to the amount of efficient investment physically possible, and although it can itself be increased through further investment, it does effectively limit the rate of development possible, particularly in the short run. Maximum absorptive capacity may, of course, permit of a higher rate of investment than that allowed by the ability of the population to save. In this case, it would be the role of an ideal international policy to fill the gap and to raise investment to the highest level consistent with absorptive capacity. On the other hand, where absorptive capacity is below the practicable rate of savings, both national and international policies should be directed towards raising such capacity. These policies would then constitute the initial phase of a long-term plan.

Thus, one of the logical ways to start planning the general rate of economic development is first to estimate the amount of domestic savings and capital imports that could be expected with no change in economic policies; then to calculate the rate of growth that this level of savings and investment would provide; and finally to compare it with the desired rate of growth. Usually, the ratio of saving to income is fairly stable over long periods of time, and these saving-income ratios are lower in under-developed countries (under 10 per cent) than in higher advanced countries (about 15 per cent). Any empirical estimation of this ratio must start with the observation of the rates of savings experienced by the country in the recent past. The estimates may be based on data for incomes and the savings of household, business and government, or domestic investment *minus* capital imports. It may also be possible to base the estimates on the experiences of comparable countries, keeping in mind the differences in income levels.

After estimating the current rate of savings, the crucial question will be what amount of net national output may be expected from the investment to be made on the basis of the estimated savings. A number of studies have been made on the amount of capital required to increase output by one unit per annum in each sector of the economy and for a national economy as a whole. This amount is called the "capital-output ratio," or "capital coefficient."

Available data clearly show that for a number of countries, e.g. the Federal Republic of Germany, Japan, Norway, the United Kingdom and the United States, the capital-output ratio for a national economy as a whole remains stable over somewhat longer periods at a level of 3 to 4. This fast may well be explained by complementarities of industrial activities, or it may be that the increases in the capital-output ratios in some manufacturing industries are compensated by decreases elsewhere, possibly by external economies due to better transport or organization of the economy. Even though there are variations, it is perhaps one of the most useful parameters with a fair degree of stability. For post-war years the coefficient was found to be 2.6 for Ceylon, 2.3 for India, 4.7 for Japan, 2.3 for Malaya, etc. A better use of already existing idle capacity may have been responsible for the low values found for Ceylon, India and Malaya. These values can be expected somewhat to rise in the future. Since, moreover, the capital coefficients differ so much from one industry to another, and, in some cases, from one technique to another, it is conceivable that capital-output ratios will change in the future, depending upon the industrial structure of the economy and on the techniques to be chosen. Nevertheless, fairly reliable estimates of capital-output ratio can be made for most countries.[1] If exact estimates are difficult, the maximum and minimum values of possible estimates may be taken, and some alternative rates of development calculated.

This capital-output ratio may be considered, at this stage of our programming, as a tentative figure, and may be adjusted later as improved information, based on detailed sectoral studies, becomes available.

Although the capital-output ratio is usually calculated as the "average" capital-output ratio, what really matters is the "marginal" or "incremental" capital-output ratio: we need information on the capital required to *increase* the national output. If we want to increase output by 20 and estimate the capital-output ratio as 4, then the required addition to the capital stock, to be provided by new investment, is 80. Evidently the figure 4 in this example stands for the "incremental capital-output ratio."

Given estimates of the current rate of savings and the capital-output ratio, the rate of economic growth, in terms of national output, could be projected in the following way. If the current level of national output is 1,000, and the saving ratio is 0.06, domestic savings

[1] One may wonder if it is safe to assume that national output is proportional to (or a linear function of) capital only. In general, national output would be technically related to the employment of labour and capital, and this relation would change through time. To base the projection of national output mainly on the capital-output ratio implies a certain type of technical change in the relevant future. There are some other econometric models, such as the Douglas function, which may be usefully applied to some countries. Details of this type of possible formulations are omitted from the text here.

would be 60, which may be invested to generate the increased national output. With a capital-output ratio of 4, this amount of savings and investment could generate an increase in national output of 15, not more. An increase in national output of, say, 20 will not be possible, because the amount of investment required for this purpose is 80, which exceeds the current savings of 60. Hence, the increase in output warranted by the savings of 60 is $60 \div 4 = 15$, which gives the growth rate of 1.5 per cent in national output. The rate of growth in national output can thus be calculated by dividing the saving ratio by the capital-output ratio.

This method of projecting the future level of national output can be checked by other ways of forecasting, e.g. extrapolation of past figures. If the projected national income shows a lower growth rate than actual income did in the past, it may be that the saving ratio has been under-estimated or the capital-output ratio over-estimated.

TABLE I — RATE OF ECONOMIC GROWTH IN TERMS OF NATIONAL OUTPUT

National output (1)	Saving ratio (2)	Saving (3)		Investment (4)	Capital-output ratio (5)	Increase in national output (6)
1,000	0.06	60	=	60	4	15

$$\text{Growth rate (G)} = \frac{(6)}{(1)} = \frac{15}{1{,}000} = \frac{(2)}{(5)} = \frac{0.06}{4} = 0.015$$

If the ratios are right, a slowing down of economic growth must be expected. Another check would be to divide the projected national output by the numbers in the active labour force, to obtain an index of the average productivity of labour in the future. If this index does not rise as much as the past trend, the estimates of parameters should again be reconsidered. If they are correct, inefficiency or unemployment must be expected in the future, unless measures are taken to prevent them.

The rate of growth of an economy will be somewhat less than shown by the preceding calculations, if the gestation period of the investment envisaged is large. The calculation above tacitly assumes that capital created by the investment in one period can be used productively in the following period. If, however, the gestation period of some investment project is longer than one year, say three years, then capital available for the productive use will not increase before three years. At that time, the level of national income will be higher, and hence the rise in production, as a percentage of total national income, is somewhat less. This means that the extension of the gestation period has the same effect as the decline in the saving ratio, or the increase in the value of the capital-output ratio. If this is the case, then the rate of economic growth computed in the preceding way must be adjusted downward. Needless to say, a lengthening of this time lag has further adverse effects, owing to the additional postponement of the fruits of investment.

If such projections of current trends show no significant rise in the people's standard of living, there is a definite need to increase the growth rate of national output. Suppose that the expected population increase is 1.5 per cent a year, the saving ratio 6 per cent, and the capital-output ratio 4. This will leave the standard of living unchanged, and represents the minimum rate of investment as defined [above]. If the *per capita* national income must increase by, say, 2 per cent a year, the national income must increase by $1.5 + 2.0 = 3.5$ per cent every year. This means that, with the same capital-output ratio, the savings ratio must be increased from 0.06 to 0.14, requiring a considerable adjustment in policy measures. If such a sudden rise in the saving ratio is difficult to achieve, the targets for improvements in living standard must be lowered to what was called . . . the practical maximum rate of investment.

A. K. CAIRNCROSS

The Role of Capital in Economic Progress*

THERE is general agreement that, in all countries, the process of economic growth and capital accumulation are closely interconnected. It was in terms of this interconnection that the earliest theories of economic development were formulated; and in the work of modern economists, output is still assumed to be limited by capital, whether

* From A. K. Cairncross, *Factors in Economic Development* (London, 1962), pp. 111–14. Reprinted by permission of George Allen & Unwin Ltd.

there is abundant labour or not. A high rate of capital formation usually accompanies a rapid growth in productivity and income; but the causal relationship between the two is complex and does not permit of any facile assumption that more capital formation will of itself bring about a corresponding acceleration in the growth of production.

In industrial countries this is only too obvious. Capital formation may assume forms, such as house-building or an addition to liquid stocks, that are unlikely to add very perceptibly to productivity although they may yield a sufficient return to make them worth while. If all capital formation were of this character, or represented an enlargement of the capital stock with assets broadly similar to those already in existence, it would be hard to account for the rates of growth actually recorded. A moment's reflection will show that even an average return of 10 per cent to capital in a country saving 10 per cent of its income annually would raise income by no more than 1 per cent per annum.[1] Similarly, efforts to impute the recorded expansion in industrial production to the additional labour and capital contributing to it invariably leave a large unexplained residue.[2] It is necessary, therefore, to take account of other influences, such as technical progress and improvements in social and economic organization, which may operate through investment, or independently of it, so as to raise the level of production. These influences, if they take effect uniformly throughout the economy in competitive conditions, will tend to swell the national income without raising the average return to capital, the extra output slipping through to the consumer, the wage-earner or the government.

How far it is correct to attribute an expansion in output to high investment, when high investment is only one of the factors at work is necessarily debatable. It would certainly be legitimate if capital formation was lagging behind, and finance could be identified as a bottleneck in the process of expansion. It might also happen that the rate of technical advance was itself controlled by the scale of investment, not merely because capital formation was the means by

[1] This point is developed in my "Reflections on the Growth of Capital and Income" (*Scottish Journal of Political Economy,* June 1959). See also the comments by E. Lundberg, "The Profitability of Investment" (*Economic Journal,* December 1959).

[2] See, for example, W. B. Reddaway and A. D. Smith, "Progress in British Manufacturing Industries in the Period 1948–54" (*Economic Journal,* March 1960) and O. Aukrust, "Investment and Economic Growth," *Productivity Measurement Review,* February 1959.

which new techniques were adopted but also because high investment created an atmosphere favourable to experimentation and innovation. There is undoubtedly some tendency for all the symptoms of rapid growth to show themselves simultaneously. But there is no invariable independence of growth on a high rate of capital formation and it is easy to imagine circumstances in which efforts to increase capital formation may actually slow down the progress of the economy.[3]

Moreover there is some justification for turning the causal relationship the other way round. If income is growing fast, investment opportunities are likely to be expanding correspondingly fast, so that the growth in income draws capital accumulation along behind it. The biggest single influence on capital formation is market opportunity, and many types of capital accumulation are likely to be embarked upon only when income is booming. If capital formation does not respond, its failure to do so will certainly act as a drag on the expansion in output. But there is no reason why it should bring it to a halt, and, given a re-arrangement of the investment pattern, income might grow a long way before the shortage of capital became acute. In the meantime the rapid growth in income, particularly if it were accompanied by high profits, would be likely to generate additional savings and so mitigate any symptoms of capital shortage that manifested themselves.

All this presupposes that a spurt in income could precede an acceleration of investment, and that capital formation is subordinate to other elements in the process of growth. These suppositions are not altogether extravagant. Technical progress does not always involve high net investment: indeed it may permit of a *reduction* in the stock of capital or an expansion in output without any comparable investment. A change in the pattern of investment could also, by enforcing the continued use or overloading of old types of plant, make possible a far more rapid construction of those newer types which bear the fruits of technical progress in greatest abundance.

Attempts are sometimes made to settle the issue by citing the apparent constancy of the capital-income ratio and deducing from this the "neutrality" of technical progress. But the capital-income ratio is affected by so many things other than technical progress: the distribution of consumers' expenditure between capital-intensive and labour-intensive products; indivisibilities in past investment—for example, in the transport and communication network; changes in the pattern of trade; investment in social assets such as roads, schools,

[3] The ground-nuts scheme in Tanganyika is an extreme example.

and hospitals to which no income is imputed; and so on. Even if these influences, too, are neutral and if the capital-income ratio does remain constant — and neither of these assumptions seems well-founded — the fact that capital and income grow at the same rate tells us nothing about the causes of growth in either. There is no reason at all why one should rule out the suggestion that the same circumstances that favour rapid growth of income are also favourable to a rapid growth of investment.

This may seem a rather arid and irrelevant issue: arid, because if capital requirements must keep pace with the growth of income that is all we need to know for practical purposes; irrelevant, because the issue relates to experiences in industrial rather than pre-industrial countries. But when it is so commonly urged that countries will be able to take-off if only they are provided with sufficient capital from outside, the issue seems neither arid nor irrelevant. For this thesis assumes the very causal relationship that is in dispute.

JOHN KENNETH GALBRAITH

Economic Development in Perspective*

IN THE YEARS since World War II, in the absence of any overall consideration of the conditions of economic advance of the kind that was offered a century earlier, we have made two assumptions. They are:

(1) That the world is divided between developed and underdeveloped countries. In the developed countries economic progress is more or less automatic — or in any case it is easily within the powers of the country itself if it follows an intelligent economic policy.

* Reprinted by permission of the publishers from John Kenneth Galbraith, *Economic Development in Perspective* (Cambridge, Massachusetts: Harvard University Press), pp. 6–16. Copyright, 1962, by John Kenneth Galbraith.

Development is possible in any underdeveloped country. It requires the provision of certain missing components.

(2) These missing elements, on the identity of which there is a good deal of agreement, are modern technical knowledge or know-how, capital, specially trained manpower, and a sound plan for using capital, manpower, and technical knowledge. If these are provided there will be progress.

The standard prescription for economic development proceeds directly from this diagnosis. Technical assistance is obtained from abroad. Steps are taken to increase the supply of domestic savings and of capital from both domestic and foreign sources. Men are sent abroad for training. A five-year or seven-year or ten-year plan is devised.

This action will indeed be sound if the diagnosis of the development problem is sound. If that diagnosis is unsound we will be having a good deal of waste motion in the world. It is my unhappy feeling that the diagnosis leaves a great deal to be desired. That it is more nearly valid for India than for most other countries can be of only limited comfort even in India, for the task of overcoming poverty and privation is one that lies on the conscience of all mankind. Let us look at the present diagnosis in the context of some practical cases.

We have said that capital and technical knowledge are the missing elements. But in many of the newer African states national government is still in its beginning stages, and in parts of Latin America is has never been brought to a minimal level of efficiency. Under these circumstances investment, whether public or private, is subject to the risks, uncertainties, and eccentricities of poor public administration. It is idle to imagine that good development plans can be created or carried out without a good government to do it. And neither technical assistance nor trained technicians do well, or are even much needed, where administration is indifferent or bad. The best agricultural scientist cannot make much headway as adviser to a nonexistent ministry. The finest tax authority goes to waste if the minister does not believe in collecting taxes, does not want to do so, or has an overly developed feeling for his friends. The first task here is not to get capital or technicians but to build competent organs of public administration.

In the last century nothing occupied a more prominent place among the requirements for economic and social advance than public education and popular enlightenment. In the new states today, or the older ones without developed systems of popular education, one also wonders if schoolbooks should not come before machine tools. Popular education releases the energies not of the few but of the many. And it opens the way to technical knowledge. Literate people will see the need for getting machines. It is not so clear that machines will see the need for getting literate people. So under some circumstances at least popular education will have a priority over the dams, factories, and other furniture of capital development.

Finally, in many countries any serious look at the larger system must soon come to focus on the shortcomings of the social order – on arrangements under which wealth and political power are a monopoly of a small minority of the population and the masses, accordingly, are excluded from all incentives to improvement. Even the most eloquent agricultural extension expert cannot explain the advantage of growing two grains of wheat where but one flourished before if the peasant knows full well that both will go inevitably to his landlord. The best-considered forms of agricultural investment or the most sophisticated techniques of agricultural extension are worthless if the cultivator knows out of the experience of the ages that none of the gains will accrue to him.

In short, on even the most preliminary view of the problem, effective government, education, and social justice emerge as critically important. In many countries, in diagnosing the barriers to advance, it is lack of these that is of critical importance. And it follows that until these barriers are removed little will come from capital investment and technical assistance. While plans may be big on paper they will be small in result.

I have said that the present diagnosis of the causes of underdevelopment, with its stress on capital, technical assistance, and planning, does not fit a country such as India too badly. India has an effective government; there is a substantial measure of literacy; she has a backlog of administrative and entrepreneurial talent; there is a solid commitment to the goals of social justice and social progress. At the same time the propensity to consume is high and the rate of saving is low, and the problem of capital supply is especially serious for that part which must be obtained from abroad. Under these circumstances attention has naturally been focused on the question of financial support to investment.

We have here an important reason for our misapprehension of the problem of development. India is by far the largest and most popular of the underdeveloped countries, China apart. Her development has attracted more attention than that of any other country partly because she has the most competent planners and the most articulate journalists and professors. India also has, despite their shortcomings, the best statistics, and, as all economists know, it is difficult to mount much of a discussion of development of a country where even imaginary gross national product data are unavailable. As a result the world has come, in far greater degree than has been realized, to identify development as a whole with the experience of India, or, more accurately, India and Pakistan. Since capital and technically trained manpower are the limiting factors in these lands they are assumed to be the limiting factor everywhere. Since competent planning is possible in India and Pakistan it is assumed to be possible everywhere.

The United States has also been responsible for some of the overemphasis on capital and technical know-how and talent. As a nation we have a healthy respect for money and its uses. And in the United States economic accomplishment depends not on the changing will of the government, not on winning the right social climate, not on finding literate workers, for these are available and assumed. Accomplishment depends on finding the capital and recruiting the engineers, scientists, and technicians. The world, in short, has generalized from the experience of the Asian subcontinent and we have generalized from our own. Those who praise cooperation in these matters should observe that it extends even to misleading students of economic development.

What is the lesson? It is not that capital or technical assistance or technical training are unimportant or that planning is a waste of time. India, where these are vitally important, is competent proof to the contrary. The lesson is that we can no longer have one diagnosis of the cause of underdevelopment. Rather we must have the particular diagnosis which fits the particular country. And in few cases will the causes of backwardness or the requirements of progress be quite the same.

More specifically we must recognize that economic development is a process[1] – one that extends in range from new nations of Africa but slightly removed from their tribal structure to the elaborate economic and social apparatus of Western nations. At each stage along this continuum there is an appropriate policy for further advance. What is appropriate at one stage is wrong at another.

[1] Although his stages inevitably invite debate, Professor Rostow's signal contribution has been in moving consideration of the problem of development dramatically in this direction. (*The Stages of Economic Growth,* Cambridge, 1960.)

In the early stages it undoubtedly involves the building of organs of public administration and the provision of an educated minority, a nucleus of people who can build the system of public administration and, for that matter, everything else. Then comes the task of popular enlightenment. This enables the masses of the people to participate in economic activity. And it opens men's minds, as they can be opened in no other way, to new methods and new techniques. Apart from its cultural role, popular literacy is a highly efficient thing. Needless to say, it is also the mainspring of popular aspiration. As such it adds strongly to the desire for development.

If development is to depend on popular participation, then there must be a system of popular rewards. There can be no effective advance if the masses of the people do not participate; man is not so constituted that he will bend his best energies for the enrichment of someone else. As literacy is economically efficient, so is social justice.

As one proceeds along the line, other requirements enter, and, depending on population and resource endowment, these will be different in different countries. Capital becomes the touchstone of development, the limiting factor, only in countries that are well along the line. Indeed, there is a distinct possibility that capital provided to countries in the earliest stages of development will be wasted. Only in a relatively sophisticated stage of development can it be well and wisely used in any considerable quantity.

At the last stop along this line are the so-called developed countries. In these—the United States, the United Kingdom, the USSR, Germany, France—capital ceases to be the limiting factor. Development becomes dependent on a complex of forces—scientific and technical skills and imagination, quality of working force, ability to make full use of available resources, clarity of national goals—which need not concern us here. . . .

. . . India's present need for capital is based not on a low level of development. It is the result, as compared with the other new nations, of a relatively high level of development that enables her to use capital effectively. It is only at this stage, where consideration must be given to how scarce investment funds can be most effectively used and where different uses of capital must be horizontally integrated and phases over time, that planning becomes very complex. We could make no more serious mistake than to imagine that the kind of planning that is done by India or Pakistan is essential for nations in all stages of development. In earlier stages it is neither necessary nor possible.

PART TWO

REQUIREMENTS AND SOURCES OF CAPITAL

INTRODUCTION

Availability of large sums of capital does not guarantee growth. But no nation can achieve a satisfactory standard of living for its inhabitants unless it can acquire substantial sums of capital with which to raise the total product of its land and labor. Thus, putting aside the other dimensions of the needs of developing nations, the acquisition of capital becomes a preeminent need. The first two questions to be asked are then: how much is needed and from where can it be obtained?

A less gloomy prognosis than that offered by some recent writers[1] is presented by Hla Myint, who questions the validity of stable capital output ratios in underdeveloped countries. Where there are possibilities of technological progress, economies of scale and increased agricultural production with small doses of capital could keep the capital/output ratio fairly low. Besides, the savings rates in poor countries, he suspects, are higher than usually assumed by economists. Comforting as these thoughts may be, they do not diminish the need on the part of the poor countries for high rates of saving and capital formation.

Using the imperfect yardstick of an international comparison of per capita incomes as a measure, the enormity of the problem—of the magnitude of necessary capital accumulation—can be appreciated quickly. If a country has a per capita income of $100 and a growth rate of 7 percent per annum in real terms, almost 30 years

[1] E.g., Robert Heilbroner, *The Great Ascent* (New York: Harper and Row, 1963), pp. 139–142.

will be necessary for that country to achieve an average per capita income of $800. Eight hundred dollars is less than one third of the United States national income per capita in 1964. This simple arithmetical example is optimistic. It assumes a very respectable rate of growth to be maintained over a protracted period *and* it assumes no increase in population. Even so, the example suggests that from a greater than subsistence level of income, the process of attaining a level of income which can be characterized as barely adequate, will take the best part of a working lifetime. At a growth rate of 5 percent per annum in per capita income, the level of $800 would be reached only after approximately 42 years. This is a formidable task. If the problem of high rates of population growth is superimposed upon the analysis, the task begins to look hopeless—at least within the lifespan of anyone now living in an underdeveloped country.[2] Once the prospect of no significant improvement in a lifetime becomes a reality, despite crash programs of capital formation, popular support for the program and for the government becomes hard to muster.

Increased savings come, Tangri argues, not from reductions of current consumption but from gains in productivity not entirely eroded by increased consumption. To the extent there exists a huge body of technical knowledge unabsorbed by a poor nation, this knowledge can provide a trigger whereby capital is accumulated. Tangri outlines the implications of incremental capital/output ratios characteristic of many development plans for the marginal rates of saving needed to outpace population growth. Next, he discusses the sources of internal private and public savings and the techniques available to society for mobilizing these savings.

Historically some nations such as England and Japan have developed without much outside capital. The Japanese case is perhaps unique. The government played the most active developmental role by manipulating rather than superceding the price mechanism.[3]

To the extent that capital is defined as "the net acquisition of

[2] An approximate measure of the effect of population growth on per capita income growth – growth in national income being predetermined – can be made by subtracting the rate of population growth from the rate of growth of national income. The example then becomes quite pessimistic.

[3] Gustav Ranis, "The Financing of Japanese Economic Development," *The Economic History Review* (April 1959), pp. 440–454.

future resources achieved at the expense of foregoing current consumption," the source of capital will be difficult to find if life is at a subsistence level. Clearly, little if any current consumption can be foregone in a subsistence economy so the source of capital becomes a vital consideration. There is, however, nearly always some possible source of saving—otherwise, as Gustav Ranis points out, the nation is not underdeveloped, it is doomed. "Happily, most of the world's low income areas are not 'doomed' in this sense. Reserves of productivity usually do exist somewhere in the underdeveloped economy; the prime problem of development is to gather them in and utilize them efficiently." He then proceeds to illustrate his argument by documenting the success story of Japan's development.

It is possible, however, that the initial saving for the society can be done by some foreigner. This occurs when the rate of capital accumulation is increased through imports of foreign capital or outright gifts of foreign aid. There are several reasons that virtually preclude complete reliance on this sort of capital. The lending nations tend to require some evidence of indigenous improvement; and nationalistic pressures within the recipient nation operate to reduce dependency on foreign aid and frequently to eliminate foreign ownership of the nation's natural resources. However, foreign aid and capital imports can be extremely valuable marginal contributions in the process of capital accumulation. With this restraint in mind Prebisch examines the Alliance for Progress program of American aid to Latin America and argues that, "Latin America . . . cannot repeat or imitate the historical course of the capitalistic development of the most advanced countries." Stressing the role of the Alliance in promoting national and international efforts of man "to dominate the forces of the economic and social process" so as to free men from poverty and exploitation, he warns that the Alliance is no magic which can obviate the need for hard and patient work.

Howard Ellis points out that of ". . . more than $60 billions expended on foreign aid programs since the war, not more than 5 percent, or about $3.3 billions has been economic aid for underdeveloped countries" amounting to about $0.25 per capita per year for the peoples of some 75 countries. Indicating the potential multiple effects of foreign capital, he advocates a substantial increase in the economic aid given by the U.S. to the underdeveloped countries.

HLA MYINT

Aggregate Capital Requirements*

WITH the idea of capital as the "missing component" of economic development which prevailed in the earlier post-war period, it was natural that economists should try to make estimates of the aggregate capital requirements of the developing countries, globally[1] and for each individual country. The most influential formula for an individual country was that it should save and invest not less than 10% to 12% of its national income. This was one of the three conditions for the "take-off" laid down by Professor W. W. Rostow, and Professor W. A. Lewis put forward his well-known dictum that "the central problem in the theory of economic growth is to understand the process by which a community is converted from being a 5 per cent to a 12 per cent saver—with all the changes in attitudes, in institutions and in techniques which accompany this conversion."[2]

What was not clearly explained was that this formula can be arrived at in two significantly different ways. Professor Rostow's argument is based mainly on the historical analogy with the advanced countries in their take-off phase in the past, during which they had not only saved and invested more than 10% of their national income but, what is more important, *held on* to this high rate of saving and investment for two or three decades. It is a part of the intense economic effort which a developing country should make to launch itself into the take-off process which involves sharp and *discontinuous* changes in the production structure. On the other hand, the formula may also be arrived at by using the *stable* overall capital-output ratio on the Harrod-Domar growth model designed for the later "mature" phase of the advanced countries after they have taken-off into steady growth. If the population of an underdeveloped country is growing at 2% per annum, its total national income must also be growing at

* From Hla Myint, *The Economics of the Developing Countries,* pp. 90–101. Reprinted by permission of Hutchinson Publishing Group Ltd., and of Frederick A. Praeger, Inc.

[1] For the earliest and most well-known example of global calculations see United Nations Report on *Measures for Economic Development of Underdeveloped Countries,* 1951, Ch. 11, Table 2.

[2] W. A. Lewis, *Theory of Economic Growth,* pp. 225–6.

2% per annum to maintain its per capita income at the same level. If it is further desired that on humanitarian or political grounds, the per capita income itself should be raised by 2% per annum, then the total national income of the country should be growing approximately at 4% per annum. Now assume that in order to obtain an extra £1 worth of income the country requires to make an investment of £3, averaging out the different capital requirements between the different sectors of the economy – that is to say, its overall incremental capital-output ratio is 3. In order to raise the per capita income at the target rate of 2% per annum, requiring a 4% rate of increase in total income to take into account population increase, the country should be saving and investing $3 \times 4\% = 12\%$ of its national income each year.

Many writers have urged the developing countries to save and invest not less than 10% to 12% of the national income without explaining whether they are giving this advice (i) on the basis of the take-off theory implying sharp discontinuous changes in the production structure, or (ii) on the basis of a stable capital-output ratio implying a process of continuous steady economic growth. They shift freely between these two approaches, ignoring the fact that the "take-off" phase (i) is separated by many decades of development from the "mature" phase (ii). Nor have they been troubled by the fact that neither (i) nor (ii) might be applicable to many of the underdeveloped countries which are still at the earlier "pre-take-off" stage.

(i) After our analysis of the earlier stages of the development of the money and the wage economy, we should now have a clearer appreciation of the fact that the underdeveloped countries are at very different stages of general economic development. A few of the relatively more advanced among them, such as India, Mexico or Brazil, may be somewhere within striking distance of the "take-off" phase. But many more of them are still in the various stages of building their runway for the take-off. In particular, they lack the basic political, "social and institutional framework" which both Professor Rostow and Professor Lewis would regard as the essential preconditions of the take-off. For instance, some of the underdeveloped countries are not yet able to maintain efficient law and order, whereas Professor Cairncross has reminded us, "most countries that have staged a successful take-off have enjoyed an antecedent period of domestic peace which prevented the periodical destruction of physical assets and gave security to investment."[3] Further, one of the less clearly appre-

[3] A. K. Cairncross, *Factors in Economic Development*, p. 120.

ciated aspects of Professor Rostow's theory is that, according to the historical examples he has given, a successful take-off requires not merely raising the saving and investment ratio above 10% of national income but maintaining it at that level for two or three decades. This requires a much higher ability not only to mobilize saving but also to invest it more effectively than the underdeveloped countries with their weak administrative, fiscal and monetary framework can be expected to have. Some of them with a high ratio of export to national income have been able to raise their saving ratio to the 10% level for a time during export booms, mainly by taxing the foreign trade sector which is easier to tax than the domestic sector. But they have not been able to sustain the process, and a considerable part of their windfall gains tends to be frittered away in inflation or prestige projects.

This, of course, does not mean that because countries are at the earlier stages of general development, they should not try to increase their rate of saving and investment. There are obvious fields: improvements in transport and communications alone can absorb a great deal of capital, both foreign and domestic. Again there are the "pre-investments" in health, education, training and research, designed to increase "human capital" and improve the country's capacity to absorb further investment. But nevertheless it is important to recognize that a country's progress towards economic development cannot be judged simply by an overall ratio of saving and investment to national income without taking into account the qualitative and less easily measurable factors such as the efficiency and honesty of its administration, the degree of its political and monetary stability, or the skills and attitudes of the people. Nor is it wise to apply a mechanical rule-of-thumb which only represents one aspect of the take-off theory to all the underdeveloped countries at different stages of the pre-take-off period.

(ii) One obvious objection which can be made to the method of calculating the aggregate capital requirements of the underdeveloped countries on the basis of a stable overall capital-output ratio is that this implies the assumption of constant returns to scale for the expansion of the economy as a whole. This assumption is justified for the mature phase of the advanced countries to which the Harrod-Domar growth model is intended to apply. For these countries, primary production, which is subject to diminishing returns, forms a small part of their total output. Besides, technical progress and economies of scale are "built in" to their economic life so that we can expect the forces for increasing returns to counteract the forces for diminishing returns. This is in fact confirmed by the advanced countries' experience of a steady and self-sustained process of economic growth for many decades. In contrast, one of the most well-established propositions about the underdeveloped countries is that agriculture and primary production forms the larger part of their national outputs and that *given unchanged techniques* the pressure of population increase on their given natural resources will result in conditions of diminishing returns to scale for the expansion of the economy as a whole.

This is as old as the Ricardian theory of the stationary state. It will be remembered that in the Ricardian theory, investment is looked upon not as the addition to the durable capital equipment, but mainly as the addition to the wage-fund or the subsistence-fund to be used to maintain a large number of workers. The rate of profit on investment is measured by the difference between the marginal product of labour in agriculture and its wage rate (both measured in terms of the "corn" or the general subsistence fund). As investment increases and more workers are put to work on the land, with given techniques the marginal product of labour will fall until it is equal to its wages. At this point, the rate of profit on investment falls to zero. This tendency to a declining rate of profit in agriculture is transmitted to the rest of the economy, particularly to the manufacturing sector, in the following way. Because of diminishing returns the rate of expansion in the agricultural output tends to lag behind that of the manufactured goods. This will raise the price of foodstuffs and raw materials in relation to the price of manufactured goods, and so raise the cost of living for the workers employed in the manufacturing sector. In order to maintain the same real wage level, therefore, their money wages will have to be raised proportionately to the rise in price of subsistence goods and this will lead to a decline in the rate of profit on investment in the manufacturing sector. Once the general rate of profits has fallen to zero, there will be no further incentive to increase investment and the economy approaches the stationary equilibrium.

In the language of the balanced growth theory (see Chapter 8) the Ricardian stationary state is brought about by the failure to expand the agricultural sector in a "balanced growth" relation with the manufacturing sector, turning the intersectoral "terms of trade" against the manufacturing sector. In the language of the capital-output ratio approach this means the diminishing returns which raise the cost of food for labour which enters into the production of the intermediate goods and capital goods will result in an increasing overall capital-output ratio as the economy expands. That is to say, we cannot apply the assumption of a stable overall capital-output ratio to the underdeveloped countries unless we can show at the same time how to counteract the general tendency towards diminishing returns. This becomes even more important when we remember that in many of these countries diminishing returns is not merely a matter of an increasing population pressing on a *given* amount of natural resources; the total available amount of natural resources is itself progressively reduced over time, because of overutilization and depletion through soil erosion, deforestation, or lowering of water tables, for example, not to mention the normal using up process of the mineral resources. In the language of the growth models, the assumption of a stable overall capital-output ratio for the underdeveloped countries requires not only that a continual stream of innovations is taking place, but that they are of a land-saving character, enabling a progressive substitution of capital and labour for natural resources.

In spite of this objection, the concept of an overall capital-output ratio has enjoyed a considerable vogue and it is frequently defended on the ground that it offers a useful basis for testing the consistency of the desired target rate of growth in national income and the available resources of a developing country. But in practice, we cannot get very far in testing the economic development plans of a country unless we are prepared to go behind the overall ratio into the structural factors which determine it.

The national income or output is not a homogeneous thing but is made up of different goods and services, each having widely varying capital-output ratios. The sectoral capital-output ratios are very high for some items, notably transport and communications and public utilities. Next in order of high capital-output ratios come housing and capital-goods industries. Manufactured consumers' goods industries together with other distributive and service industries generally have lower capital-output ratios.[4] The capital-output ratio in the agricultural sector of the underdeveloped countries is generally likely to be low, although some of the big irrigation and river valley projects

[4] W. B. Reddaway gives the following sectoral capital-output ratios for the third Indian five-year plan which has adopted an overall capital-output ratio of 2.2: Agriculture, 0·9; Mining and Manufacturing, 2·6; Small Industries and Construction, 1·0; Railways and Communications, 6·5; Housing, 18·0; Other services, including Schools, Hospitals and Roads, 2·0. *The Development of the Indian Economy,* p. 211. It may be noted that Housing, Railways and Communications have a very high capital-output ratio. In other countries, electricity generation and supply tends to have a very high capital-output ratio (cf. S. A. Abbas, *Capital Requirements for the Development of South and Southeast Asia,* pp. 140–4). It may also be noted that, in general, manufacturing and mining industries require a relatively modest share of total investment, about a quarter of it, while the share of housing can be quite as much (cf. Colin Clark, *Condi-*

require vast sums of capital. Characteristically, the expansion of agricultural output in these countries depends not only on capital inputs such as fertilizers and improved equipment, but also on improvements in technical knowledge, marketing, credit, or land tenure, for example, which are not directly reflected in the capital-output ratio.

Now the overall capital-output ratio is nothing but the average of these different sectoral capital-output ratios weighted according to the quantities of the different goods and services which are to be produced. Thus, before we can calculate the overall ratio we must specify the proportions of the different constituent items which are to make up a proposed rate of increase in the national output. But this barely scratches the surface of the problem of testing the consistency of an integrated economic development plan. For one thing, the target figures of increase in outputs of various items are not given independently of each other. Many of them are required not only for final consumption but also as intermediate goods or inputs in the production of other items. In testing, therefore, the consistency of the target figures of items and the resources available for them, we must take into account not only the direct requirements but also the indirect requirements of capital. Further, these complex input-output relationships should be tested not only for a given year, but continuously over the whole period of the plan. This means that for each of the intervening years, say, during a five-year plan, the rates of expansion of the different sectors must be phased so that they dovetail into each other, without any sector lagging behind their concerted timetable and holding up the others. For if this happens, shortages and excess capacities will develop and this will alter the effective capital-output ratios in the sectors which have gone out of alignment with the general plan. By the time we have gone through the consistency of an integrated development plan in this way, it does not help us much further to "sum up the whole thing" in the form of an overall capital-output ratio.[5]

tions of Economic Progress, third edition, pp. 604–5). The difficulties of calculating the sectoral capital-output ratios arise not only from paucity of statistical information but also from conceptual difficulties. Thus the high capital-output ratios in transport and communications should be counterbalanced by the economizing of capital stocks and inventories in other sectors, notably in commerce and distributive industries. Then there are doubtful borderline cases like fertilizer production which can be put either in the agricultural sector or in chemical industries.

[5] W. B. Reddaway, *The Development of the Indian Economy,* Appendix C, for a further discussion of this concept.

Yet a great deal of importance has been attached to this ratio, and the real reason seems to be that it offers a convenient shorthand basis for making out the case for increasing economic aid to the underdeveloped countries. From our arithmetical example it will be seen that with a typical population growth of 2% per annum, assuming a conventional capital-output ratio between 2 and 3, a target rate of growth in per capita income between 2% and 3% commonly adopted on humanitarian grounds will require a saving-investment ratio of about 10% to 12% of national income. In the early 1950s, it was generally accepted that the underdeveloped countries were too poor to save more than about 5% of their national income. Hence the need for massive injections of outside capital to fill this gap.

Since the early 1950s, many economists have been moving away from their simpler views of the "capital shortage" of the underdeveloped countries based on calculations of aggregate capital requirements and overall capital-output ratios. There are many reasons for this.

First, there is now a greater recognition of the fact that a developing country's ability to save does not depend only on the level of its average national income but also on other factors such as the pattern of income distribution, the ability of the government to mobilize savings through taxation and the ability of the financial institutions making up the capital market to mobilize private savings. Many economists still work on the basis that the chief source of private savings in the underdeveloped countries is the ploughing-back of profits; that is to say, only the capitalists save and the landlords do not. But Professor Cairncross has pointed out that this may underestimate the important role which the development of the capital market can play in mobilizing private savings and that in the British historical experience at least, a considerable proportion of these savings have come from the landowning classes.[6] Whatever the precise reason, it is interesting to note that the more recent writings on the underdeveloped countries tend to put their average saving ratio at 7% of their national income instead of the conventional level of 5% widely adopted a few years ago.[7] There is also a growing realization that some of the developing countries may be suffering

[6] A. K. Cairncross, *Factors in Economic Development,* pp. 125–8. It may also be pointed out that the real reason why capital accumulation comes to a stop in the Ricardian stationary state is not because landlords are less thrifty than capitalists, but because with a zero rate of return on capital, no one has any incentive to increase saving.

[7] P. Hoffman, *One Hundred Countries and One Quarter Billion People,* and GATT *Report of International Trade 1959;* also Cairncross, op. cit., pp. 53–5.

not so much from a shortage of savings in general as from the shortage in supply of particular types of goods which they need to import from abroad. This special shortage of foreign exchange as distinct from a general shortage in savings can be particularly acute for a country like India with a low ratio of export to her national income and a poor prospect of expanding her exports sufficiently to meet the rising burden of debt service payments on further borrowing.

Next, there is the remarkable fact that since the early 1950s, the idea that the rich countries should help the poor countries has become more firmly established in international opinion than earlier writers dared to hope. As Dr. W. H. Singer, himself a notable champion of increasing aid to the underdeveloped countries, has pointed out: "in the past five or six years the flow of resources to the underdeveloped countries by the medium of public aid has been a more dependable element in the flow of foreign exchange and resources to the underdeveloped countries than either export earnings, service payments, flow of private capital or any other balance of payments item. Foreign aid has steadily and year by year increased at a rate of 15% per annum from $2 billion around 1954 to around $3½ billion now (1960) without a single setback in any year."[8] Dr. Singer feels that it is time to advance beyond the simpler generalizations about "capital shortage" which have served their purpose in rousing public opinion in favour of international aid. Many economists will now share this feeling — a feeling which is strengthened by experiences in some underdeveloped countries where a considerable proportion of aid has been wasted owing to defects in organization and lack of capacity to absorb capital. Thus there has been a considerable shift in emphasis from injecting a massive dose of investment in the form of material capital, to investment in "human capital." Education is now increasingly regarded as the "missing component" of economic development.

Finally, at the theoretical level, many economists are now concerned not merely with making pro-rata calculations of capital requirements on the basis of given capital-output ratios but with the further

[8] H. W. Singer, *Recent Trends in Economic Thought on Underdeveloped Countries* (mimeographed November 1960), p. 31. Dr. Singer's figures are based on the United Nations' definition of "economic aid" which excludes short-term loans and private investment, but includes long-term loans on commercial terms from international bodies such as the World Bank and from national governments. Adopting a broader definition, Mr. A. Shonfield puts the total public and private aid to the underdeveloped countries in 1958 at a figure of $5½ billion; *The Attack on World Poverty*, Appendix I. Cf. F. Benham, *Economic Aid to the Underdeveloped Countries*, Ch. 2, for a good discussion of the problems of defining "economic aid."

problem of whether these ratios themselves represent the most economical way of using capital in relation to the other factors of production in the underdeveloped countries.

SHANTI S. TANGRI

Saving and Economic Development*

ONE of the first important steps in development is not to cut consumption (for increasing saving) but to increase output through (i) more efficient use of existing techniques and employed resources, (ii) productive utilization of unused resources (land, labor, capital and knowledge), and (iii) increased intra-national and international division of labor.

The next step is to prevent the whole of the increased output from being used up for current consumption (either for supporting the existing population at a higher standard of living or for sustaining a larger population). A sustained increase in per capita incomes requires a rising level of per capita savings and investment which in turn requires a faster rise of the per capita marginal rate of savings. Most poor countries of today are supposed to save around 5 per cent of their national income, barely sufficient to replace their depreciating capital. In most of these countries new investments are of a nature as to result in marginal capital/output ratios of 3 or more. For every increase of 1 per cent in national income, 3 per cent more of the national income must be invested. Thus to match the rate of growth of Western countries (about 3 per cent annually) they need to save about 14 per cent of their income (including 5 per cent for depreciation). In order to achieve this average rate of savings in

* From "Patterns of Investment and Rates of Growth" by Shanti S. Tangri, pp. 18–21. Unpublished Ph.D. dissertation, The University of California, Berkeley, 1961.

about a decade it can be shown that they need to step up their marginal rate of saving to as high as 33⅓ per cent immediately and maintain it there. And if population expands at about 3 per cent annually, per capita incomes will remain constant while, because of the increased rate of saving, per capita consumption will continue to fall until it becomes stabilized at about two-thirds of its former level. If average savings are less than 14 per cent, per capita consumption would fall still further. To prevent it from falling then, much higher rates of marginal and average saving are needed. To the extent that the population growth rate is less than 3 per cent in an underdeveloped country, its massive capital needs for holding per capita income or consumption constant, are diminished. Population growth, however, tends to accelerate in the initial phase of economic development. Success in raising per capita income in this phase has thus to depend, quite heavily, on increasing output per unit of capital, enough to generate increased saving after meeting these consumption demands.

Increased saving can be voluntary on the part of recipients, or it can be extracted out of them by government or private organizations through fiscal, monetary, marketing, and administrative measures like price-manipulation, inflation and taxation, or expropriation. Where incomes originate in the public sector, large shares may be retained by government at the source. Voluntary (private) savings can increase if the mass of people acquire a desire for greater material gains coupled with the willingness to abstain from the using up of these gains for raising consumption standards or larger families, or if increased incomes go to those who have a high propensity to save. This involves a widening of income inequalities as the marginal propensity to save tends to be higher among the higher income groups.

The first alternative involves a concerted campaign of propaganda, and social education or indoctrination. If successful, this technique of increasing voluntary savings creates the least political discontent. It necessitates a whole set of complementary economic and social measures, like the creation of a network of institutions to mobilize small savings. An essential ingredient in such a program is a development program which uses local resources and benefits local people visibly and in a relatively short period of time.

The second technique, i.e., increasing savings by increasing income-inequalities, is politically unpopular. Where the mass of people have no or little political power (as in eighteenth-century England, nineteenth- and early twentieth-century Japan, and twentieth-century Russia and China) this process has been freely adopted.

The climate of mid-twentieth century is one of antipathy to high profits and income inequalities. Landlords can often be taxed without adverse political or economic consequences, but white and blue collar workers and farmers are difficult to tax politically. Entrepreneurs are easy to tax politically — but this creates, generally, adverse effects on savings and investment in the private sector. In such a situation investors want to take their capital out of the country. This is often made difficult by governments. However, the inflow of foreign capital, if any, diminishes. Native businessmen may continue to save and invest as before, if they believe that failure to do so may give impetus to political trends more hostile to their interests and particularly if alternative economic opportunities, inside or outside the country, are equally or more restricted.

Any decline in private savings needs to be compensated by increased governmental savings and capital formation. Finding it difficult to increase taxes, governments turn to a hidden form of taxation, viz., inflation, for diverting resources from current consumption to investment. Whatever be the effects of inflation on savings and capital formation, its political effects are not pleasant. Inflation hurts mostly the urban middle classes which are vocal and articulate. Inflation also hurts wage earners whose wages lag behind prices. Wage-increase demands spread from one sector of the economy to another resulting in much industrial strife and disruption of production. Organized unions and a vocal middle class and other fixed-income groups become sources of political tensions — more so if inflationary tendencies continue to increase rather than diminish. The groups which definitely benefit from it, the entrepreneurial and investing classes, are generally politically unpopular among the mass of people. The redistributive effects of inflation can thus become a major source of political protest. If, meanwhile, population is growing as rapidly as income, inflation can raise savings only by depressing living standards of many people, swelling the ranks of political malcontents.

Finally, the gap between growing output and consumption can be widened by governments' appropriating a share of increased production in agriculture and industry, before it accrues to workers or owners (of land or capital). Good and acceptable improvement taxes can be built into development programs. But, quite often, taxes and tax collectors appear on the scene after development measures have borne fruit and find tax-collection rather difficult. In industry it is difficult for government to convince workers that they should not demand wage increases commensurate with increased productivity.

Workers may accept wage restraints however, if similar restraints are put on entrepreneurial and managerial groups.

RAÚL PREBISCH

Economic Aspects of the Alliance for Progress*

THERE are many in Latin America who for years have been advocating the need for profound changes in our economic and social structure to pave the way for an accelerated pace of economic and social development. . . . For them the recognition accorded in the Charter of Punta del Este to the urgent need for these changes constitutes an event of far-reaching importance.

Indeed, the basic ideas underlying this document were conceived and gradually developed over a period of years in Latin America. For a long time we have constantly maintained the view that a vigorous movement of industrialization was imperative in the process of development. We have also reaffirmed the inevitability of land reform and other changes in the social structure, in order to facilitate the massive adoption of modern technology and the progressive redistribution of the fruits of development. We called attention to the importance of the terms of trade, and the need to counteract their tendency to deteriorate through transformations in the economic structure; and we insistently advocated measures to attenuate their fluctuations. The idea of the Latin American Common Market emerged in our countries. And the need for a considerable enlargement of foreign funds to supplement a more intense mobilization of internal resources in order to accelerate the rhythm of development, was also preached for a long time from Latin America. . . .

However, there has developed a rather peculiar tendency to

* From Raúl Prebisch, *The Alliance for Progress,* ed. John Dreier (Baltimore, 1962), pp. 24–65. Reprinted by permission of the Johns Hopkins Press.

present these ideas as having been conceived in the United States, or as constituting a ready-made American blueprint to be applied in Latin America. I am really concerned about this trend, for not only is it contrary to the facts, but its political implications are highly detrimental to the Alliance itself and to the broad popular support it requires in Latin America.

Latin America has to project its own image—its authentic image—in this process of development. We have to shape it according to our own ways of feeling and thinking and our own concepts of action. We cannot repeat or imitate the historical course of the capitalistic development of the most advanced countries. Consequently, we have to find our own path with our own creative powers. Naturally, this does not preclude intellectual influences from outside. On the contrary, we expect them; but these influences should be only an element—though a very important one—in the elaboration of our own system of thinking, helping to guide us in our efforts to act upon the economic and social process. . . .

STRUCTURAL OBSTACLES TO THE PENETRATION OF MODERN TECHNOLOGY

The possibility of extirpating poverty and its inherent evils in Latin America as well as in the rest of the developing world is no longer a utopian idea. Indeed, the role of modern technology is to make it feasible. However, the rapid and balanced spread and assimilation of modern technology entail greater efforts that require, and must be accompanied by, those profound changes in the economic and social structure to which I referred earlier. Several structural obstacles are retarding or interfering with the orderly penetration of modern technology. I would like to clarify briefly the nature of these obstacles. . . .

Industrialization and Import Substitution

Industrialization constitutes an outstanding expression of the changes needed in the Latin American economic structure. The reason for its need, although very clear and simple, has frequently been subject to misunderstandings within and without this region. Due to the evolution of production techniques as well as of consumer demand, when per-capita income increases persistently owing to the absorption of modern technology, the demand for industrial products grows at a much faster pace than the demand for primary products.

If this greater demand for manufactures could be fully met by imports from the industrial centers in exchange for foodstuffs and primary goods exported to them at satisfactory prices by Latin America, then this region's need to industrialize would not be so urgent. However, given the fact that the industrial centers also experience similar changes in the composition of the demand as per capita income increases, consumption and imports of Latin American primary goods grow very slowly. The protectionist policies followed by some industrialized countries in order to safeguard their own production, particularly in the agricultural sector, further restrict imports of Latin American origin.

Moreover, thanks to the constant advances in manufacturing techniques, the industrial centers – either through better utilization of traditional raw materials and their by-products or the replacement of these by synthetic materials – need and employ a decreasing proportion of imported raw materials for their industrial production. Consequently, Latin American industry must develop so as to satisfy the demand for manufactured goods that the region can no longer afford to import.

Industrialization and the Absorption of Manpower

This then is one of the important dynamic roles of industrialization. The other is the absorption of manpower released from the agricultural and other sectors of the economy as technical progress penetrates into them. Yet, even in those Latin American countries where the rate of industrial development has been rather high, the absorption of available manpower has been far from satisfactory. Large segments of the manpower force remain unemployed or underemployed, and this is one of the causes for persistent social tensions.

This phenomenon is caused by two main factors: first, the high rate of population increase; and second, the nature of modern technology. . . . While we have a scarcity of capital and potentially abundant manpower, we are indiscriminately introducing production techniques conceived for and applied in advanced countries where the prevailing conditions are just the reverse. In the more advanced countries, technology is directed more and more towards economizing manpower; and this is the same technology which is available to countries in the course of development.

Labor-Saving and Labor-Absorbing Investments

. . . The progressive adoption of the technology of the large countries, because it economizes manpower, also necessitates a faster rate of economic growth. If this rate is low, the maladjustments resulting from shifts in the labor force will be greater. People will be shifted from occupations that are turning away workers before the occupations that can be expected to absorb manpower are in a position to do so. This leads to a congestion or a surplus of unemployed or under-employed manpower which, in addition to representing a waste of factors of production, may understandably lead to social tensions. . . .

The Dynamic Elements of the Population

A low level of capital accumulation and a slow growth rate produce not only stresses of the kind just described but equally, if not more, have important effects on social mobility and the emergence of dynamic elements of the population.

Each generation has its dynamic elements, which usually place their distinctive stamp upon it. There are individuals who are destined to play a decisive part in economics, technology, scientific and cultural matters, politics and trade unionism. In economics and technology, their task will be to organize and direct enterprises, initiate action, and assume risks and responsibilities. It is towards these persons that the drive for technological levelling-up, to which I shall refer later on, should be directed.

Such individuals constitute dynamic elements not only because of their special gifts but also because of their active role in promoting social mobility. A high rate of economic growth hastens this process, which in turn influences the growth rate. Hence the strategic importance of these dynamic elements. An annual growth of per-capita income of only one per cent, as is now the case, or of three per cent, not only determines whether the standard of living will be doubled within 70 years, or within less than 25. It also means something else of vital importance: the higher of these two rates will permit the rapid absorption into economic activity of these dynamic elements, broadening their horizons, whereas a moderate rate means the waste of a great part of these forces and mounting tensions which, if they fail to find an adequate outlet in economic activity, will eventually discover some way of bursting out of the economic and social bonds that contain them. . . .

THE BASIC FLAWS IN INDUSTRIALIZATION

. . . The process of industrialization suffers from three main flaws, which have weakened its contribution to improving the standard of living. These are: first, all industrialization activity is directed towards the domestic market; second, the choice of industries to be established has been based more on circumstantial reasons than on considerations of economic yield; and last, industrialization has failed to overcome the external vulnerability of the Latin American countries.

The excessive channelling of industry toward the domestic market is a result of the development policy pursued in the Latin American countries and of the lack of international incentives to exports of industrial goods from the region.

Development policies have been discriminatory as regards exports. Assistance has been given – through tariffs or other restrictions – to industrial production for internal consumption but not to industrial production for export. The production of many industrial goods has thus been developed at a cost far above the international level, when they could have been obtained with a much smaller cost differential in exchange for exports of other industrial products which might have been produced more profitably. The same could be said of new lines of primary commodities for export and even of traditional export commodities within certain relatively narrow limits. . . .

As regards the second flaw in industrialization – the frequent absence of considerations of economic yield – this is largely due to the lack of a far-sighted policy, which was naturally very difficult to establish at a time when the countries of Latin America had little experience in that respect. The process of industrialization has been neither continuous nor regular. Pressure of circumstance has provided a strong impetus to it, for example, in times of import difficulties due to a scarcity of foreign currency or to the consequences of the World Wars.

On such occasions, restrictions were applied where they were easiest to introduce without upsetting the development of the internal economy, namely on imports of finished items, particularly consumer goods. Thus, industries producing such goods sprang up. The easiest course of action, however, is not always the most economic. In many instances the production of certain raw materials, intermediate industrial goods, or capital goods would have resulted in a lower cost differential with respect to the international market than was the case with consumer goods.

The combination of the first two defects in the industrialization process leads to the third: failure to strengthen the structure of the Latin American economy so as to withstand external fluctuations and events. For want of a proper division of labor in industry – as also in agriculture – the policy of import substitution has had to go much further than would have been necessary otherwise; and as the preference in respect of import substitution fell on consumer goods, this trend either ended, or is about to end, in almost complete substitution as regards such goods in the more industrially advanced countries of Latin America. Imports are thus confined to the raw materials and intermediate goods essential for maintaining current economic activity, and also to capital goods.

This has brought about a new kind of vulnerability resulting from the disappearance of the reducible margin of imports. When exports decline cyclically, inability to import essential goods has an unfavourable effect on the growth rate and even leads to a contraction of the economy.

Excessive Protectionism and the Latin American Common Market

From another angle, industrial protectionism has been exaggerated. Of course, protection is indispensable for industrial development, but in Latin America, generally speaking, excessive trade barriers have isolated industry from world markets, and thus it has lacked the advantages of healthy foreign competition.

This and the relatively small size of national markets have been frequently responsible for internal restrictive or monopolistic practices, which weaken the incentive to technological progress and the corresponding increase in productivity. As a consequence we frequently see in Latin American countries forms of concentration of economic power that are not the result of technical evolution, as in the case of advanced countries; on the contrary, they very often only hamper it.

Not always do our countries give recognition to the principle that free initiative and free competition are inseparable. I hope that the formation of the common market will introduce an element of sound competition through the gradual lowering and elimination of customs duties between the Latin American countries, and eventually lead to the lowering of duties vis-à-vis the rest of the world.

We envisage a broad, single market instead of the twenty watertight compartments in which Latin American industrialization is taking place at present. . . .

Strengthening the Latin American Common Market

. . . One of the basic aspects of the organization of the common market consists precisely in the establishment of agencies to give more forceful technical and financial support to Latin American private enterprise under the common-market system, irrespective, needless to say, of whatever each individual government wishes to undertake directly in the field of industry. . . . At Punta del Este the governments recognized that Latin American private enterprise must be given the strongest possible international support, from both the technical and the financial angles, so that it can gradually reach levels similar to that of its foreign counterparts. The tendency in question, which is general and must now be given concrete expression, is dictated not by an anachronistic form of nationalism but by factors whose roots lie very deep. Economic development is basically a process of training and perfecting national aptitudes in respect to technique and production. We should do well to remember that one of the aspects of the Soviet method of economic development which, despite the system's immense political and social cost, seems to exert a powerful fascination over our younger generations may be summed up in the following principle: whatever a country's point of departure, however great its technical backwardness, and however unstable its economy, it now appears possible that in the space of a single generation unsuspected technical abilities can be developed, if the population of such a country is subjected to a strict and systematic process of technological training. Modern technology has no longer any secrets. Even formerly primitive countries have learnt to grapple with all the manifestations of modern production techniques, from the extraction of petroleum and the exploitation of natural resources to the most complex patterns of industrial technology. . . .

The Latin American common market will reduce production costs and will eventually facilitate Latin American exports of manufactures to the most advanced industrial centers of the world. This movement will require a more liberal foreign trade policy on the part of these centers in relation to exports from developing countries. The greater our traditional exports and the exports of industrial goods in which we have comparative advantages, the larger will be our own imports of other industrial goods whose production in Latin American countries would still be relatively costly in relation to the levels prevailing in the more advanced industrial centers.

This expansion of international trade would have, therefore, an implicit element of reciprocity. I hope that the industrial centers will find it possible to grant trade concessions to exports of manufactures from developing countries without asking from them in return such concessions as might weaken their industrial development.

THE LAND AND ECONOMIC DEVELOPMENT

. . . Industrial development is complementary to the introduction of technical progress in agricultural activities. However, the system of land tenure that still prevails in most of the Latin American countries is one of the most serious obstacles to economic development. But the problem must not be looked at from one side only. Efficient use of the soil depends not only upon the reform of the land tenure system, but also upon the rate of economic growth itself. . . .

Marked Disparities in Land Tenure

The land tenure system is characterized by extreme inequality in the distribution of land and of the income accruing from it. Most of the productive land is in the hands of owners of large estates, relatively few in number, and the remainder is distributed among innumerable small and medium-sized holdings that are usually too small to permit rational farming practices. Moreover there are large numbers of people without any land at all.

Some of the large estates are, of course, farmed efficiently. But as a general rule, because of their very size, their owner draws a substantial income without troubling himself to improve the farming of his land or encourage his tenants or sharecroppers to do so. Moreover, he has only to wait, and the value of the land will increase by virtue of the growth of the population and the development of the economy. And this in itself helps to attract those whose object is not rational farm management but a means of protecting themselves against inflation or of evading wholly or in part the burden of progressive taxation.

The stronger this interest in the opportunistic investment possibilities of the land — rather than in making the best use of its productive potential — the greater will be the disproportion between its value and its immediate yield. And this puts it almost out of reach of those who are best qualified to work it. Herein lies one of the reasons for the existence of minifundia. The existence of large estates, the excessively high price of land and the shortage of resources inevitably foster this phenomenon, as the pressure of population on the available land increases.

Land and Population

The dissemination of modern production techniques is also very uneven. Progress has been made in respect to production for export in particular but not in respect to agricultural commodities in general. Low productivity continues to characterize production for domestic consumption. This is one of the most important strongholds of pre-capitalism. There is no other field in the Latin American economy in which the profundity and magnitude of the disequilibrium between labor and capital are more apparent. In Latin American agriculture, there is still a high proportion of the active population working on the land on a basis of scanty capital and very low productivity per capita and per unit of area. . . .

Modern Agricultural Techniques and Development

The rate and pattern of economic development strongly influence the use of the land. The rate helps to determine domestic demand for agricultural commodities and the speed at which the population surplus is absorbed. The pattern affects the incentives to agricultural production. Both factors set a limit to the introduction of modern farm techniques and the expansion of production.

There are some branches of agricultural production in which demand has grown rapidly and has given the consequent impetus to technical progress. This has been true mainly of production for export and of import substitution activities. The farmer has surmounted the obstacles created by the land tenure system or has sought new land which he has worked on a basis of advanced and capital-intensive techniques. But in the remainder of the agricultural sector, which comprises most of the rural population, the situation has not been the same. Demand has grown more slowly here than the demand for other goods and services, and it has not been vigorous enough to overcome the difficulties confronting it.

To remedy this, state action to improve the use of the tax system, to redistribute the land, to disseminate techniques, and to furnish the necessary capital for their application was essential. Such action has not been taken on a scale proportional to the magnitude of the problem. Even the relatively slow increase in demand referred to has often had to be satisfied by increasing imports or reducing exports or their rate of growth, with the consequent aggravation of foreign trade disequilibria.

Thus, the limit to the introduction of up-to-date techniques is set not only by demand but also by the capacity of the rest of the economy to absorb the rural population surplus.

This same duality is also apparent in the case of technical progress, which tends, on the one hand, to increase the yield per unit of area and, on the other, to reduce the labor force required per unit of product. The logical limit to the advance of technology is set, in one instance, by demand and, in the other, the absorption capacity of the economy.

Redistribution of the Land and Surplus Labor Force

Redistribution of the land pursues the following two basic objectives: to relieve social tensions by improving the distribution of property and income; and to increase productivity by creating conditions favorable to the introduction of modern techniques.

Carried out on rational lines, redistribution alone may result in an improvement in productivity, since giving more land to those who have little, by making use of land left idle or badly farmed, offers immediate opportunities for an expansion of production. From this standpoint, it would seem essential to consider the position with respect to those latifundia which are efficiently operated. However well the land is worked, there is a dimensional limit beyond which productivity, instead of increasing, is liable to decrease. Within this limit, there would be no reasons to divide up the land, since other efficacious means exist of redistributing the income it produces.

But this applies only to a few large estates, and these as a general rule are not common in agriculture for domestic consumption, where the prevalent type of farm is characterized by highly unsatisfactory techniques and waste of productive land.

It is here that the problem of technical improvements and population arises. The greater the extent to which modern techniques are introduced, the larger will be the population surplus that must be transferred from the land to other activities; and the bigger should be the share of land assigned by redistribution to each active person remaining in the agricultural sector. In the case of countries which, historically speaking, have only recently been settled, the problem is relatively simple; and within a few years the manpower surplus in question may be productively absorbed by the economy if the rate of economic development is improved.

But the same is true of only a small proportion of Latin America's agricultural population. As regards the remainder, the existing surplus is striking in its proportions, despite the low prevailing level of technology. Technical progress would of course greatly reduce manpower requirements even if production were to expand at a rapid rate.

This raises the most serious aspect of the whole question of redistribution. The active population, at present redundant – and this is all the more true of that which technical progress would create – can only be employed very slowly and gradually in the manpower-absorbing activities if the rate of economic development is not intensified considerably.

The foregoing assertion is valid from the standpoint of the economy as a whole. As far as individual farms are concerned, it may well happen, and often does, that the capital used to curtail manpower requirements generates a notable increase in profits. The situation described is yet another manifestation of the discrepancy between advanced technology and the lack of resources for its assimilation. . . .

This is a problem which agriculture cannot solve by itself. Capital is required in order to economize on labor in agriculture as in other activities; and it is also needed if that labor is to be absorbed without lowering the current productivity levels of the activities absorbing it. If sufficient capital for this latter purpose is lacking, it will have been worse than useless to expend capital on saving labor which is to be left without employment or at best employed unsatisfactorily.

In such cases, priority will have to be given, in agricultural research and in the dissemination of sound farm practices, to those techniques which increase the yield per unit of land, although in some cases the two types of technique are closely related.

Nor could this line of action be pursued without taking into account the growth of demand. Otherwise, the benefits deriving from technical progress would be lost to agriculture. It would not matter if this were to happen in the domestic market, provided always that producers retained a sufficient margin to encourage further investment. But if the transfer were external, a situation unfavorable to development would recur.

In other words, the capital available for economic development, and the proportion of the population that will have to remain on the land, constitute decisive elements in determining the size of the holdings which will have to be formed by dividing up large estates or combining small ones, with due regard to ecological conditions. This, of course, sets a limit to the application of labor-saving techniques.

EDUCATION AND TECHNICAL TRAINING

Other important transformations of the social structure in addition to land reform are indispensable to the full penetration of technical progress and the best use of human resources. Indeed, one of the most apparent manifestations of the anachronistic economic and social constellation prevailing in Latin America is the very small proportion of people from the lower social strata having opportunities for medium and higher education. This constitutes a formidable obstacle to social mobility, with a tremendous waste of human abilities, vital energies, and initiative.

We frequently stress in Latin America the spiritual values of western culture and the essential role of individual initiative in economic life, and I of course agree with this. But if one examines matters closely, one cannot escape the conclusion that at present only a relatively small fraction of the population has actual access to that culture and enjoys the possibilities of fully exercising their individual initiative. . . .

I have been asking myself insistently if the inherent shortcomings of the Soviet system of centralization of economic decisions have not been largely compensated by the active selection of men promoted by their methods of education and training. I am tempted to imagine the enormous results that we could obtain in Latin America if we could radically transform our educational systems in the light of our own experience and that of others in this field. . . .

THE REDISTRIBUTION OF INCOME AND THE ACCUMULATION OF CAPITAL

It is not necessary to explain how these changes in the economic and social structure will bring a better distribution of income. . . . The consumption of the higher-income groups must inevitably be restricted so that economic and social investment may be increased. But it is inconceivable that a redistribution policy could be applied for the purpose of directly and immediately raising popular levels of consumption without some sacrifice of such investment. The end in view can only be progressively achieved as per-capita income rises and its distribution is improved. What is required to increase it is precisely the expansion of investment by means of the above-mentioned combination of resources.

Even so, the progressive redistribution of a growing income cannot bring about a parallel increase in popular consumption. The upward trend of the latter must be slower than that of income, so as to raise the rate of investment until the level necessary for the maintenance of a satisfactory rate of economic development is reached.

Popular Capital Formation

Herein lies the most difficult aspect of the problem, in which a new approach is more vital than it is in other cases: how to augment capital formation as the pattern of income distribution changes.

Without capital formation on the part of the broad masses redistribution policy will have adverse effects on economic development. . . .

Origin of Major Disparities and the Problem of Coping with Them

As regards redistribution, in the course of capitalist evolution it has resulted from two forces, in addition to the economy's own momentum: the organization of the trade unions and taxation.

The power of the trade unions is increasing considerably in the Latin American countries. But in some of them it is not yet effective enough to ensure that wages are adjusted correlatively to the increase in productivity. What is more, it has not been possible to correct the adverse effects of inflation. Here, in the last analysis, is to be found a very serious manifestation of the relative abundance of underproductive manpower in primary activities, artisan industry, and unskilled services. Its persistent pressure tends to preclude a rise in real remunerations.

But the reverse has occurred in some cases, where the trade unions have wielded their power in order to raise wages above the point warranted by productivity and the entrepreneurs' profits. The results has been the inflationary spiral, with all its pernicious and disturbing effects.

Incentives to Capital Formation

These circumstances partly determine the action of the rate and place a greater responsibility upon it when the weakness of the trade unions leaves income distribution almost completely dependent on the free play of economic forces.

Through taxation the state may exercise a considerable influence over income distribution and capital formation. But, on the whole, it cannot be said to have made good use of its opportunities. In some cases, taxes have clearly come to form a high proportion of the economy's aggregate revenue, but only a relatively small part of the resources thus obtained is assigned to capital investment, the remainder being used to cover current expenditure in which social objectives are not always given the priority they deserve.

From another point of view, it is unusual for the high-income groups to contribute as fully as they should, either because the tax system is regressive or because tax evasion makes a mockery of taxation itself or of proper tax collection.

Furthermore, fiscal interests seem to have prevailed over economic considerations. Although investment is insufficient, the proportion of income that is consumed receives the same tax treatment as the proportion that is allotted to investment. Nevertheless, some reforms have been introduced with a view to stimulating investment and discouraging consumption on the part of the higher-income groups. This is an avenue which calls for thorough exploration.

It is undeniable that this tax differentiation intends to rectify disparities in consumption but not in the capital formation deriving therefrom. The inheritance tax is of course the ultimate corrective.

When the state, instead of taking this course, resorts to taxation in order to appropriate resources for investment, this does not mean that it is obliged to use the whole amount directly. The use of part of such resources for promoting private action through development institutions has proved to be effective in several countries. But no assistance has been forthcoming in this connection from international sources except on a very small scale. Nonetheless, Latin American private activity offers great opportunities for absorbing those resources through these or other suitable channels.

The loan of investment resources as a means of promoting the eventual formation of capital does not have to be confined to enterprises. It may also be extended to workers. This may turn out to be one of the most effective means of achieving popular capital formation and a question arises here which should be given some consideration. The use of credit for the purchase of durable consumer goods has been rapidly gaining ground in the Latin American countries. This is clearly a way to afford the broad masses of the population access to goods which it would be difficult for them to obtain in any other way. But this, in common with inflation, is a grave threat to saving practices. Perhaps such practices could be encouraged by credits for the purchase of securities by the workers themselves, either in the enterprises in which they work or in others. These possibilities should be explored and the organizations that finance development might play a very important part in these new aspects of industrial democracy.

Loans for capital investment have so far been made direct to enterprises. A substantial part could be made indirectly, that is through loans to workers for the purchase of securities. Reference has already been made to the need for international credit institutions to devote a large part of their operations in Latin America to encouraging incentive on the part of firms and concerns in the area. These operations could be co-ordinated, in one way or another, with the growing participation of workers in the capital formation process.

The Latin American countries regularly face a very serious problem of capital formation in their public services. The use of international assistance for the purchase of securities in these services could have very important repercussions on the accumulation of capital and on the management of the enterprise. The participation of the producers and users of such services could provide a new way out of the common dilemma of choosing between foreign ownership and management by the state.

THE IMPORTANCE OF COMBINING INTERNAL AND EXTERNAL RESOURCES

. . . A great effort has to be made in Latin America to mobilize internal resources . . . these efforts need to be much more intensive than is commonly supposed. If the investment required to accelerate development, with due allowance for the remarkably rapid rate of growth of the population, is considered in conjunction with the claims of education, housing, and public health, among others, the resulting figures will certainly exceed, perhaps in unsuspected measure, the internal investment resources that are being deployed at the present time. The greater effort thus needed implies a radical change in patterns of consumption, especially among the higher-income groups.

But the internal effort must be supplemented by an inflow of international resources much greater than that made available in the past. Otherwise, the rate of domestic investment would have to be greatly intensified, and this would mean imposing extremely severe restrictions not merely on the income of the more privileged groups, but also, I greatly fear, on the consumption and consumption increments of the broad masses of the population, to the point where very heavy political and social hardship might be involved.

That this restriction of popular consumption is possible is clearly shown by the experience of the Soviet system of economic development, but this experience also shows clearly its political implications. I have grave doubts that this policy of restriction of popular consumption can be maintained past a certain point within the present institutional framework. For the further one presses in that direction, the greater the need to employ measures of a coercive type, and the more they are applied the harder it will be to preserve the democratic system and institutions. . . .

THE POLITICAL SIGNIFICANCE OF THE ALLIANCE FOR PROGRESS

It is here, in my view, that we find the fundamental significance of the new policy of international co-operation embodied in the Alliance for Progress. Foreign funds brought into play in accordance with its provisions and principles should not be construed as an instrument to constrain the sovereign orbit of the great national decisions of Latin American countries, influencing their free determination with regard to internal or external matters. Otherwise, this would simply mean the dissolution of the Alliance. . . .

The Alliance for Progress is . . . an instrument through which the acceleration of economic and social development can be made perfectly compatible with the improvement of the democratic process in Latin America. . . .

Internal and External Resistances

Let us not minimize the strength of the forces opposing the efforts aimed at giving a real economic and social content to the Latin American democratic systems. It would be greatly misleading to think that the acceptance of structural reform by Latin American governments at the Punta del Este Conference has paved the way for their easy and immediate implementation. However, let us not minimize, either, the effects of persuasion. Before the commitments contained in the Alliance were subscribed, it was hard to conceive the immediate possibility of some Latin American countries' entering into land and tax reform. However, these reforms are being prepared now, though not always with great determination. In some cases, the ruling circles understand the unavoidable need for these and other reforms and will act accordingly. In other cases, there is apt to be stern resistance. If this happens, then there is no other course but to continue untiringly the persuasive work until such time as progressive forces willing and determined to introduce these economic and social reforms finally prevail. Then the time will have arrived for a maximum deployment of the means of external co-operation envisaged in the Alliance for Progress.

But resistance to change is not only internal, it may come from external sources too. I am referring particularly to certain types of foreign enterprises that are an integral part of that outdated constellation of forces to which I referred earlier.

Although aware and in favor of the contribution of foreign private capital to our economic development, I am also aware of some cases where new and constructive formulas are urgently needed in this respect. I have in mind especially those cases of foreign enterprises which constitute real enclaves of an economic and technological character that are practically inaccessible to the people of the country, and also those other cases where they exert an undue influence in the national life.

Foreign Private Enterprise

The role of foreign private capital should be appraised not only from the standpoint of its direct effects on the national product, but also with respect to its contribution to the transfer of technology through the training of local staff at all technical levels. Considerable progress has been made in this field. The old method by which the country concerned provided only natural resources and labor, while foreign private enterprise had a monopoly of technique and management, is largely disappearing, although it still has some strongholds. Otherwise, initiative from abroad is usually an effective means of training domestic skills.

However, close examination reveals that foreign private investment has by no means reached the level that might have been expected in Latin America. Furthermore, much of this investment continues to be concerned with the exploitation of natural resources and with public services rather than with industry or farming. Yet it must not be inferred that the solution of the problem lies simply in encouraging investment in the last two types of activity. This would certainly alleviate the shortage of national savings, but it would undoubtedly give rise to other problems, and signs of these are not hard to find even now in some Latin American countries. . . .

National and Foreign Private Enterprise

The technical and economic superiority of foreign private enterprise compared with its Latin American counterpart is not open to dispute, and neither is its importance in the transfer of technology. But this transfer operation is not enough; it is also necessary to encourage, in the country concerned, the training of local entrepreneurs, of men to organize and manage production, with all the attendant responsibilities. Otherwise, if a marked increase were to take place in the influx of private foreign capital, nationals of the country, because of their unfavorable position, would be unable to face the competition of their foreign counterparts either in existing fields of activity or in new branches. . . . The unequal competition might well give rise to friction and antagonism which could easily take on a political complexion.

The measures that can be taken in this direction are various. The most obvious would be the establishment of a system of credits and technical assistance for domestic enterprises, so as to reduce and eventually eliminate the inequalities of capital and technology. There is a considerable potential demand for such credit, especially if it is not made conditional upon the principle that only foreign capital may be used for imports of machinery and equipment, and if operations are adjusted to the methods current in the Latin American countries, which are sometimes different from those in other countries.

Although it is true that the Latin American countries are not in general ready for very large-scale projects, it is equally true that there are a number of more modest — although none the less important — steps that they could take if such a system were organized. The rapidity and vigor with which imports of capital goods increase during a favorable export phase is enough to demonstrate the fact that this potential demand exists and could increase enormously if a persistent effort were made to encourage it.

In most cases it would not be necessary to establish new credit institutions, since use could be made of existing ones, private or official, that are sufficiently reputable and responsible to undertake such a task without the need for detailed control exercised at the source of the funds.

In this context, it might also be useful to extend the practice followed in some countries whereby local capital is invited to associate with foreign private enterprise on equal terms, or even to contribute a major share of the investment.

In other cases, very promising results have been obtained by provision of part of the capital from foreign sources, together with contracts for services to manage the industry during its first years, until domestic management skills are developed. There have also been strikingly successful examples of industries that originated as state enterprises and eventually passed under private domestic control, with respect both to the technical side and to ownership and management.

At a less ambitious level where considerable success could nevertheless be achieved with proper organization, there have been co-operative activities of a strictly technical nature, involving concessions of the right to use certain processes and the granting of assistance against payment of royalties.

The Role of Foreign Private Capital

. . . Unless an attempt is made to bring about this gradual and progressive technological levelling-up in the broadest sense of the term, the steady advance of development will be impossible, since the patent differences in training levels and the inaccessibility of certain techniques to local personnel will breed discord. Development will be neither economically sound nor politically stable.

Herein lies the key to the solution of more than one problem, since lower standards of technology give rise to understandable inferiority complexes, whereas technological levelling-up, by strengthening the idea of equality of opportunity, will make a noteworthy contribution to the fruitful association of domestic and foreign elements in the wide field of private enterprise. . . .

THE HISTORIC RESPONSIBILITY CONFRONTING LATIN AMERICA

. . . The Alliance is a dynamic formula for co-operating with those countries determined to use their will and power to dominate the forces of the economic and social process, and not to dominate men, dictating to them, from within and without, what they must do and what they must think.

We have before us the fascinating possibility of making great strides in industrialization with ample scope for individual achievements; of bringing about land reform and technical progress in agriculture, with freedom to own land through our own efforts. We have this and much more to look forward to, for all of this has ceased to be an inaccessible goal in this world of ours. Why should we have to renounce our political freedom to reach this target? That is the question that is being asked insistently in all our countries. We must give a clear and definite answer. We must integrate in a single and coherent system of ideas, the concepts of economic development and social justice, of active democracy and personal dignity, with all their inherent prerogatives. . . .

HOWARD S. ELLIS

A Perspective on United States Foreign Aid*

I do not hesitate to say that the development of foreign nations will presumably add to our own economic well-being, and that we can contribute to our own important import and export interests by furthering foreign economic development. One of the ways in which we can do so is by grants in aid and loans to underdeveloped coun-

* From Howard S. Ellis, *Economic Development and International Trade: A Perspective,* ed. Paul Zook (Dallas, 1959), pp. 16–19. Reprinted by permission of Howard S. Ellis and Southern Methodist University Press.

tries for economic development. It would be consistent with the general argument presented here to advocate an increase of the American foreign economic aid program, and that is indeed my position. But this thesis requires several explanatory passages.

The first point is that our economic development aid has been very small indeed. Of the total of somewhat more than $60 billion expended on foreign aid programs since the war, not more than 5 per cent, or about $3.3 billion, has been economic aid for underdeveloped countries. Divided out over the 1,150,000,000 inhabitants of 75 underdeveloped countries, this amounts to approximately $3.00 per capita spread over 12 years. But perhaps this arithmetic is less significant than the simple fact that military and defense support aid was 20 times as large. This ratio does not signify to my way of thinking a correct assessment of the relative merits of winning support in Asia and Africa for the democratic nations by military and by nonmilitary devices. What would be "adequate" is, of course, a most difficult question; but the suggestion of the Committee for Economic Development of a $1 billion annual appropriation for the peaceful offensive against communism by means of foreign economic aid – about 1.5 per cent of our federal budget – can hardly be characterized as overweening.

The second point is that even a substantial increase of this order in American foreign aid would still represent a small sum, and would signify no more than a starter, a grubstake, or a spark plug for foreign programs of economic development. It represents only a small fraction of the capital which must be mustered up for development by most of the poorer nations if the rise of their national product is to go beyond the increases of population and thus raise per capita incomes. This capital, needless to say, must chiefly come from those economies themselves. Because a foreign aid program of $1 billion annually would provide about $1.00 per capita annually of investment in the less developed regions, it cannot be ascribed an affinity for "big-push" theories of development, which sometimes imply that if only sufficient capital is forthcoming, other elements in the difficult problem of "getting off the ground" in the development process will quickly fall into place. In fact, progress in the poorer countries, as in the richer ones, is compounded of a number of essential elements and no one in isolation can perform a magic transformation. Nevertheless, a small injection of foreign public capital, especially into sectors in which private capital moves very slowly, may under favorable circumstances have strong multiple effects on national income.

This multiplier effect of foreign aid could be considerably fortified — and this is my third point — if somewhat more attention were devoted to eliciting the help of private enterprise in the receiving country. Although the role of the state must be larger in Asiatic nations and in most underdeveloped countries than it is typically in Europe or North America, there is nevertheless a tendency for the governments of these poorer economies to try to do too much. Not only are these economies underdeveloped, but so are their political and administrative systems. Their capacity is limited. . . . Our foreign aid should strengthen and expand the orbit of private enterprise and the price system. One of the ways of doing so would be to provide loans to firms rather than to governments. This has been made possible on a limited scale by the International Finance Corporation, an adjunct of the International Bank, now in its second year of operation. Still more important would be the proposal recently made by the National Planning Association that the United States government make loans to private enterprises up to 75 per cent of the value of approved foreign investment in less developed countries in which the United States government has assistance programs. At the same time other measures can be taken to encourage the flow of American *private* capital, as for example through the formation of investment trust companies for holding foreign securities. The aim should be to supplement and eventually to supplant public funds for foreign development.

PART THREE

STRATEGIES OF CAPITAL ACCUMULATION

INTRODUCTION

Whether investment is defined normally or broadly, the amount of capital required per person for an acceptable living standard in any society is likely to be very large. Another aspect of the same problem is that of ensuring that the accumulation of capital in a given period actually assures the generation of more capital in the next period—this Is a question of the rate of investment and the strategy of accumulation.

Ragnar Nurske and Everett E. Hagen take opposite sides on the problem of the vicious circle of poverty and the lack of sufficient incentive to invest. These two selections serve as an introduction to a complex controversy: can a poor nation achieve self-sustaining growth by means of the gradual accumulation of capital over a (long) period or does such a program almost inevitably retrogress after a certain time and necessitate a "big push" of investment in order to break out of the low-income trap? The gradualist (big push) argument is, in essence, not subject to conclusive proof. According to one school of thought, virtually all of the countries which have developed did so under the impetus of a big push of some kind.[1] Thus, the "big push" argument claims an historical base and "big push" development can essentially be conceived of as being equivalent to Rostow's concept

[1] This analysis may not apply to countries such as Australia and the United States, which developed extensively by incorporating capital (in the form of virgin land) almost at will and with negligible cost. Countries now in the process of developing are not able to contemplate this method of achieving self-sustained growth. Some economists argue that it does not apply to Japan or even to England.

of "take-off." Even if historical experiences of rapid development support the theses of "big push" or "take-off," one must consider the question of whether these historical experiences, resulting for the most part from combinations of basic economic forces and either *laissez-faire* practices or strong central control, may be reproduced for future generations by deliberate policy decisions.

If the gradualist argument is conceived of in terms of the Harrod-Domar model shown in Figure 1 (see the General Introduction), it can be represented as a series of periods in which society is slowly transformed. At the end of this series of periods, the shifts in the two functional relationships will have been achieved. The saving schedule will have shifted up minutely each period as a result of income redistribution and changing values on the part of the society and the capital/output ratio will have become lower in each period until both attain values which will characterize the post "take-off" economy. On the other hand, the big push arguments can be see in Rostow's terms as accomplishing shifts in the two functions of the same approximate magnitude but in a very much smaller number of periods.

The literature on balanced *vs.* unbalanced growth is growing and often confusing. The terms have different meanings for different people. The simplest and clearest meaning of balanced growth is associated with some highly abstract models of growth in which all outputs and inputs grow proportionately. The nature of assumptions and conclusions of such models (such as a constant per capita output) severely limit their relevance to the problems of development. Some writers consider "big push" and balanced growth as just two facets of the same process born of the necessity to break the low income trap. Others argue that the two theories are mutually inconsistent.

Howard S. Ellis, taking this latter viewpoint, takes a critical look at the big push theories. " 'Big push' economists," he concludes, "are generally strong interventionists.[2]. . . To harvest external economies, to overcome technological lumpiness, to induce saving or lower birth-rates they favor the forced draft of infant industry protection, or inflation, or appropriation of the agricultural surplus, or state control of investment, or exchange control, or some combination of these, including various hues of planning, socialism and communism . . . [but] countries characterized as underdeveloped economically are frequently also underdeveloped politically: Their citizens often expect

[2] Nurkse is an outstanding exception. [Editor's note.]

of these governments economic attainments far beyond their capacity. . . . The economic development of many Latin American countries in recent years has taken place despite, rather than because of, the activities of governments."

Myint relates the big push-gradualist controversy to the balanced *vs.* unbalanced growth argument. This latter argument is essentially concerned with the problem of external economies in underdeveloped nations. External economies (diseconomies) are economic benefits (costs) which are consequences of the interdependence of economic activity, for which the market system can make no allowance. Put in a nutshell, the balanced growth doctrines (of Nurkse, Ellis, and others) may be said to recommend that all sectors advance in such a fashion that neither bottlenecks nor overcapacity exist in different sectors at different times, while unbalanced growth willingly conceives of overcapacity and bottlenecks in the belief that the bottlenecks produce a stimulus to invest and overcapacity achieves economies of scale as the overcapacity wanes with the ongoing growth process. Albert Hirschman argues that imbalances set in motion market and non-market forces which start pushing the economy back toward balance, rejecting the notion "that growth has to be balanced from the start or cannot take place at all." Hirschman, a critic of balanced growth, finds himself in agreement with Ellis, a proponent of balanced growth, that the weakness of the market to deal with problems of disequilibria arising in the growth process does not warrant the assumption that governments can handle the job more satisfactorily.

But unlike Ellis, he believes that balanced economic growth puts greater demands on the scarce decision-making talents and mechanisms in underdeveloped countries than does unbalanced growth.

Others argue that imbalances are unavoidable even in a well-planned and growing economy—why *plan* them in poor economies beset by imbalances? Hans Singer reviews some of the critical features of this debate such as the time horizons of economic planning and the nature and extent of access to international markets. Rising productivity in agriculture or industry, investment in import-substituting industries, or expansion of the market by investing in the social infrastructures can provide internal markets while export promotion can secure external markets for the products of a growing economy; this, according to Singer, obviates the need to balance investment in all sectors or industries for the sake of providing balanced demand. In addition, Singer argues, "Where you start with imbalance, you need further imbalance in order to come closer to balance."

Like Hirschman, he believes that balanced growth is an expensive prescription requiring a very large package of resources—a criticism that Ellis directs against the big push doctrines.

Strictly speaking, the notion of balance in investment should refer to the concept of *pattern* or *composition* (allocation) of investment while the question of the *quantum* or *rate* of investment should be relevant to the gradualist-big push argument.

Much of the literature, unfortunately, fails to treat these two related but distinct issues separately.

RAGNAR NURKSE

The Size of the Market and the Inducement to Invest*

THE VICIOUS CIRCLE OF POVERTY

In discussions of the problem of economic development, a phrase that crops up frequently is "the vicious circle of poverty." It is generally treated as something obvious, too obvious to be worth examining. I hope I may be forgiven if I begin by taking a look at this obvious concept.

It implies a circular constellation of forces tending to act and react upon one another in such a way as to keep a poor country in a state of poverty. Particular instances of such circular constellations are not difficult to imagine. For example, a poor man may not have enough to eat; being under-fed, his health may be weak; being physically weak, his working capacity is low, which means that he is poor,

* From *Problems of Capital Formation in Underdeveloped Countries* by Ragnar Nurkse, pp. 91–96. Oxford University Press, Inc., 1953. Reprinted by permission of Oxford University Press, Inc. and of Basil Blackwell Publisher.

which in turns means that he will not have enough to seat; and so on. A situation of this sort, relating to a country as a whole, can be summed up in the trite proposition: "a country is poor because it is poor."

Perhaps the most important circular relationships of this kind are those that afflict the accumulation of capital in economically backward countries. The supply of capital is governed by the ability and willingness to save; the demand for capital is governed by the incentives to invest. A circular relationship exists on both sides of the problem of capital formation in the poverty-ridden areas of the world.

On the supply side, there is the small capacity to save, resulting from the low level of real income. The low real income is a reflection of low productivity, which in its turn is due largely to the lack of capital. The lack of capital is a result of the small capacity to save, and so the circle is complete.

On the demand side, the inducement to invest may be low because of the small buying power of the people, which is due to their small real income, which again is due to low productivity. The low level of productivity, however, is a result of the small amount of capital used in production, which in its turn may be caused at least partly by the small inducement to invest.

The low level of real income, reflecting low productivity, is a point that is common to both circles. Usually the trouble on the supply side receives all the emphasis. The trouble there is certainly obvious and serious, and some aspects of it will be thoroughly gone into later. But the possible block on the demand side, once one becomes aware of it, is also fairly obvious, though it may not be so serious, or so difficult to remove, as the supply deficiency.

Besides, let us remember that capital is not everything. In addition to the circular relationships that plague the capital problem, there are, of course, matters of unilateral causation that can keep a country poor; for instance, lack of mineral resources, insufficient water or barren soil. Some of the poorer countries in the world to-day are poor partly for such reasons. But in all of them their poverty is also attributable to some extent to the lack of adequate capital equipment, which can be due to the small inducement to invest as well as to the small capacity to save.

WEAKNESS OF INVESTMENT INCENTIVES

It may at first be surprising to hear that there can be anything wrong on the demand side of the problem of capital formation in underdeveloped countries. Can there be any deficiency in the demand for capital? Are not the backward areas, almost by definition, greatly in need of capital for the efficient use of their labour and for the exploitation of their natural resources? Is not the demand for capital in these areas tremendous? It may well be; and yet in terms of private incentives to adopt capitalistic methods in the productive process there is the difficulty that stems from the limited size of the domestic market in the early stages of a country's economic development.

The inducement to invest is limited by the size of the market. This proposition is, in effect, a modern variant of Adam Smith's famous thesis that "the division of labour is limited by the extent of the market."[1] The point is simple and has long been familiar to the business world. It is a matter of common observation that in the poorer countries the use of capital equipment in the production of goods and services for the domestic market is inhibited by the small size of that market, by the lack of domestic purchasing power, not in monetary but in real terms, in a sense to be presently defined. If it were merely a deficiency of monetary demand, it could easily be remedied through monetary expansion; but the trouble lies deeper. Monetary expansion alone does not remove it, but produces merely an inflation of prices.

This simple point, that the incentive to apply capital is limited by the size of the market, has a certain validity not only in the exchange economy of the real world, but even in the economy of an isolated individual like Robinson Crusoe, well known to our forefathers from elementary textbooks. Suppose that Robinson Crusoe had two or three hundred nails (which he got, let us say, from a wooden box washed ashore on his island) and wanted to drive them into some trees in order to hang up his fishing nets or personal effects. It would pay him first to sit down and make a simple hammer with which to drive these nails into his trees. His total effort would be reduced; he would do the job more quickly. But if he had only two or three nails it would not be worth his while to make a hammer. He would pick up and use a stone of suitable size. It would be a slow and inconvenient method; but it would be uneconomic to produce capital equipment in the shape of a hammer just for driving in two or three nails.

[1] It was Allyn A. Young who suggested this re-interpretation in his well-known essay, "Increasing Returns and Economic Progress," *Economic Journal,* December 1928 (now reprinted in *Readings in Economic Analysis,* edited by R. V. Clemence, Cambridge, Mass., 1950, Vol. I). It is easy to see, and Adam Smith recognized it himself, that the division of labour is closely connected with the use of capital in production.

In the exchange economy of the real world, it is not difficult to find illustrations of the way in which the small size of a country's market can discourage, or even prohibit, the profitable application of modern capital equipment by any individual entrepreneur in any particular industry. In a country, for instance, where the great majority of people are too poor to wear leather shoes, setting up a modern shoe factory may be a doubtful business proposition; the market for shoes is too small. Many articles that are in common use in the United States can be sold in a low-income country in quantities so limited that a machine working only a few days or weeks can produce enough for a whole year's consumption, and would have to stand idle the rest of the time. In Chile, for example, it has been found that a modern rolling mill, which is standard equipment in any industrial county, can produce in three hours a sufficient supply of a certain type of iron shapes to last the country for a year. In these circumstances the inducement to install such equipment is lacking. In some cases foreign branch plants which had been established in certain Latin American countries were subsequently withdrawn because it was found that the local market was too small to make their operation profitable.[2]

These examples may exaggerate the difficulty, but I do believe that, to some extent, the difficulty is real. To produce with more capital per unit of output means generally, though not invariably, producing on a larger scale, in the sense of a larger output per plant. This is what matters in the present context, though it may be that in a given line of production any increase in output, even when it maintains the old degree of capital-intensity, will be discouraged by the smallness of the market.

The economic incentive to install capital equipment for the production of a certain commodity or service always depends in some measure on the amount of work to be done with this equipment. Naturally the individual business man must take the amount of work to be done — the size of the market for his commodity or service — more or less as he finds it. He may hope to be able to deflect some of the present volume of consumers' demand in his own favour; but where real income is close to the subsistence level, there is little or no scope for such deflection. The limited size of the domestic market in a low-income country can thus constitute an obstacle to the application of capital by any individual firm or industry working for that

[2] For these and other examples, see G. Wythe, *Industry in Latin America* (New York, 1951).

market. In this sense the small domestic market is an obstacle to development generally.

How can this obstacle be removed? What is it that determines the size of the market? Some people may think, in this connection, of monetary expansion as a remedy, others of high-powered methods of salesmanship and advertising. Some may think of the size of a country's population as determining the size of the market; others, again, may have in mind the physical extent of the country's territory. All these factors are of secondary importance, if not irrelevant. A popular prescription is that small adjacent countries should abolish restrictions on trade with each other. But the smallness of a country is not the basic difficulty. The difficulty can exist even in very large countries such as China and India.

The crucial determinant of the size of the market is productivity. In an all-inclusive view, the size of the market is not only determined, but actually defined, by the volume of production. In the economy as a whole, the flow of goods and services produced and consumed is not a fixed magnitude. With a given population, it is a variable depending on people's productive efficiency. It is sometimes said that, if only prices could be reduced (money incomes remaining the same), the market could be enlarged. That is true, but if this were to happen it would imply an increase in productivity and real income. The market would be similarly enlarged if people's money incomes could be increased while prices remained constant. Again, this would be possible only with an advance in productive efficiency, implying an increase in real income. We are here in the classical world of Say's Law. In underdeveloped areas there is generally no "deflationary gap" through excessive savings. Production creates its own demand, and the size of the market depends on the volume of production. In the last analysis, the market can be enlarged only through an all-round increase in productivity. Capacity to buy means capacity to produce.

Now productivity—or output per man-hour—depends largely, though by no means entirely, on the degree to which capital is employed in production. It is largely a matter of using machinery and other equipment. It is a function, in technical terms, of the capital-intensity of production. But, for any individual entrepreneur, the use of capital is inhibited, to start with, by the small size of the market.

Where is the way out of this circle? How can the market be enlarged? Even though in economically backward areas Say's Law may be valid in the sense that there is no deflationary gap, it never is valid in the sense that the output of any single industry, newly set up with capital equipment, can create its own demand. Human wants being diverse, the people engaged in the new industry will not wish to spend all their income on their own products.[3] Suppose it is a shoe industry. The shoe producers cannot live on shoes alone and must depend on the exchange of shoes for the other things they need. If in the rest of the economy nothing happens to increase productivity and hence buying power, the market for the new shoe output is likely to prove deficient. People outside the new industry will not give up other things in order to buy, say, a pair of shoes every year if they do not have enough food, clothing and shelter. They cannot let go the little they have of these elementary necessities. If they *were* willing to renounce some of their present consumption in exchange for an annual pair of new shoes, these things would become available for the shoe workers to make up the balance in their consumption needs. As it is, the new industry is likely to be a failure.

The trouble is due by no means solely to discontinuities in the technical forms of capital equipment, though these will accentuate it. It is due above all to the inevitable inelasticity of demands at low real-income levels. It is in this way that poverty cramps the inducement to invest and discourages the application of capital to any single line of production. The enlargement of the market through the rise in productivity that would result from increased capital-intensity of production is inhibited by the initial smallness of the market.

The problem of technical discontinuities, in turn, is due not merely to the fact that equipment produced in advanced countries is adapted to domestic mass markets there and is not, as a rule, best suited to conditions in the poorer countries. Even if equipment were devised particularly for the latter, discontinuities would still remain. Additions to capital equipment in any case are apt to come in relatively big units, and there is especially a characteristic lumpiness in the process of investment in overhead capital facilities such as railways, power plants and water works.

While thus the technical discontinuities may call for sizable forward "jumps" in the rate of output, the small and inelastic demand in a low-income country tends to make such jumps risky if not altogether unpromising in any given branch of business considered by itself. If, in the past, attempts at jumping forward in particular branches have for these reasons come to grief, individual enterprise is

[3] See Paul N. Rosenstein-Roden, "Problems of Industrialization of Eastern and South-Eastern Europe," *Economic Journal,* June–September 1943, p. 205.

likely to take a dim view of future investment prospects; the demand for capital will be depressed.[4]

We recognize, in one of its aspects, the vicious circle of poverty. We perceive a constellation of circumstances tending to preserve any backward economy in a stationary condition, in a state of "underdevelopment equilibrium" somewhat analogous, perhaps, to the "underemployment equilibrium," the possibility of which, in advanced industrial countries, was impressed on us by Keynes. Economic progress is not a spontaneous or automatic affair. On the contrary, it is evident that there are automatic forces within the system tending to keep it moored to a given level.

All this, however, is only part of the story. The circular constellation of the stationary system is real enough, but fortunately the circle is not unbreakable. And once it is broken at any point, the very fact that the relation is circular tends to make for cumulative advance. We should perhaps hesitate to call the circle vicious; it can become beneficent.

EVERETT E. HAGEN

Vicious Circles*

Professor Hagen discusses two alleged barriers to economic development, the inability to save because of low incomes and the unwillingness to save because of the demonstration effects of high consumption levels of the developed on the less developed countries.

[4] All this is superimposed on the fact that in communities afflicted with mass poverty the qualities of enterprise and initiative are usually in short supply to start with, and that the demand for capital tends to be sluggish for this reason alone. I am grateful to Mr. Robert G. Link for a detailed comment setting forth with more precision the possible ways in which the three factors – inelastic consumer demand, technical discontinuities and lack of enterprise – can keep down the demand for capital in low-income countries.

* From Everett E. Hagen, *On the Theory of Social Change* (Homewood, Illinois, 1962), pp. 42–47. Reprinted by permission of The Dorsey Press with acknowledgment to the Center for International Studies of the Massachusetts Institute of Technology.

Both arguments lead to the theory of the vicious circle of low income and low savings. He takes issue with these hypotheses on empirical and theoretical grounds which support the alternative notion that the ratio of savings to income is more or less constant at widely different levels of income. He next turns his attention to other alleged barriers such as the insufficiency of inducement to invest (Nurkse), small size of the market (Kindleberger), and lumpiness of capital investment (Rosenstein-Rodan).

A THIRD barrier is sometimes found in another vicious circle: inadequate demand to justify investment in improved methods. More efficient plants, it is argued, have a minimum efficient capacity; because of the low level of income, the market is not large enough to provide a market for this minimum flow of output; hence there is little inducement for investment; without investment, productivity does not increase and incomes do not rise. "On the demand side," Nurkse writes, "the inducement to invest may be low because of the small buying powers of the people, which is due to their small real income, which again is due to low productivity. The low level of productivity, however, is a result of the small amount of capital used in production, which in its turn may be caused at least partly by the small inducement to invest."[1] He spells out the minimum-size plant capacity argument and cites as examples shoe production in a hypothetical economy so low that few persons wear shoes, and steel production in Chile. He might have cited other examples: electric light bulbs, aluminum, automobiles.

However, his conclusion that the national market in low-income countries is not large enough to permit production on a scale necessary for reduction in cost is false, or at least grossly overdrawn. For while there is little demand for certain products in low-income countries, it is clear beyond question that in every country or colonial area of the world except possibly a handful of the tiniest ones there are many other products commonly used in the area for which the demand provides a market amply adequate for productive units using modern methods. A few examples are sugar, rice or flour milling (depending on the tastes of the people), sandals, umbrellas, textiles, textile products, cigarettes, candies, and a considerable variety of

[1] *Problems of Capital Formation*, p. 5.

agricultural products. Even economies of two or three million persons with very low income provide markets much more than large enough to justify technological progress in the production of these and a number of other commonly used products.

As an example, the first modern sugar refinery was established in one valley of Colombia and the first modern textile mill in another between 1900 and 1910, when the population of the entire country was not more than six million and the level of per capita income, as conventionally measured, probably less than $100; and each valley was so isolated from the rest of the country by barriers to transportation that the market for each enterprise initially was confined primarily to its own valley—at a maximum estimate, one fifth of the total national market in one case and much less in the other. Both flourished, as did a stream of other improvements.

Moreover, many investments not of a highly mechanized type are appropriate and advantageous. In sum, while many investments of a type which would be profitable in the United States would not be profitable in a low-income country, on the other hand many investments which would be profitable in the latter would not be profitable in the United States. There is no clear reason to assume the presence of a greater volume of investment opportunity in one, relative to the size of the economy, than in the other.

Kindleberger refines the argument concerning the size of the market as follows: In a traditional society much production is for a local market only. A very large percentage of the goods consumed in a village may be produced within 10 or 15 miles of the village. If there is a single producer of some handicraft item, reducing his cost of production will increase his sales very little. Even in a single village, for most commodities or handicraft products there are a number of producers; but the concept of production as a family affair, not an enterprise to be expanded by reducing costs and taking sales away from competitors, may dull any incentive to ponder ways of improving methods. If improvement in transportation and changes in marketing institutions have expanded the market to a region or the country as a whole, the situation is radically altered. The producer then faces an impersonal market. If he can reduce his price or improve his product, he can take sales from 100 or 1,000 other producers; hence the incentive to improve his methods is great.[2]

From this set of facts the conclusion is sometimes drawn that if transport facilities were improved, production for a national market

[2] Concerning the importance of expansion of the market from a community to a larger area, see C. P. Kindleberger, *Economic Development,* chap. vi.

would begin and techniques would improve. No doubt there are circumstances in which this is true. With distribution costs reduced, the profitable operation of a large-scale plant is easier than otherwise, and there must be cases in which this change is just sufficient to induce someone to make the attempt and causes it to be successful.

However, to conclude that this is the central reason for failure of larger-scale plants to appear is a *non sequitur.* There may be other reasons. That there are seems likely. The developments in Colombia mentioned above suggest that a market sufficient in size to justify a large-scale plant may often be accessible to a local producer. Moreover, other obstacles, not economic in nature, are apparent.

Undoubtedly, if there were no barriers other than technical ones, for many products used in low-income countries increasing the size of the plant in which they are produced would considerably decrease costs or increase the quality of the product. However, if larger plants do not appear, a consideration apart from the size of the market or any other technical factor is probably the most important reason why they do not. The operation of a large plant involves rather radical changes in behavior, including that of the entrepreneur himself, and in interpersonal relations. A large plant will not be more economic until the management of new relationships has been mastered. I suggest that where larger plants have not appeared in traditional societies the most important reasons typically are that the community finds the change in behavior patterns involved somewhat repugnant, and entrepreneurs motivated to run against the social pressure (including their own inner reluctance) and capable of managing the nontraditional plants have not appeared. Clifford Geertz's discussion of the first budding of new entrepreneurship in two Indonesian towns, in Chapter 16 [of Hagen's book] illustrates the difficulties vividly.

THE LUMP OF CAPITAL ARGUMENT

It is sometimes asserted that economic growth can go forward only when certain types of capital known as social overhead capital or infra-structure are present. By social overhead capital is meant those types of capital goods which serve not one industry but many, and which hence provide a springboard for advance in many industries. Examples are roads, railroads, and power installations, none of which, it is asserted, or at least neither of the last two of which, can be fully effective except in large and expensive units. Economic growth is blocked because low-income countries cannot afford the large lump of investment needed to complete large projects and because the large projects are a necessary base for other projects—so the argument runs.[3]

When the expositors of this argument are asked how growth got under way in the first countries, which had no possibility of aid from the outside, they may suggest that in some, such as England and Japan, social overhead capital in transportation was provided free by the ocean; that other early investment in Britain was financed by income from her empire; and that Britain in turn, after it had begun to develop, financed transportation and other facilities in other countries.

In evaluating this argument it is necessary to distinguish among three statements: (1) that social and economic overhead capital may be fruitful in stimulating other development; (2) that at some stage in development some such projects are indispensable for further development; and (3) that the growth of present low-income countries is blocked through their inability to finance such indispensable projects.

Concerning the first proposition, there can be little dispute. The possible stimulus to other industries of transport and power facilities is beyond question. Concerning the second and third propositions, however, there is reason to be skeptical. The argument that absence of overhead capital facilities forms an insuperable or at least very serious barrier to economic growth violates the principle of continuity and flexibility in growth, which derives from general considerations of continuity in history. It is doubtful that any economic system is really so confined to only one course and order of development that its development is blocked, or even severely hampered, because very large-scale projects are not possible. There are always many alternative possible paths of change. Per capita income may be increased if a private entrepreneur or the state devises better spinning frames, introduces wheelbarrows, cultivates better seed, develops a more efficient division of labor in the production of sandals, and so on in infinite variety. An analytical model of an economy so rigid technologically that it cannot develop without some one or more large unitary projects seems too unreal to be a fruitful model for reality. It seems more realistic to assume that if a consider-

[3] See Singer, "Economic Progress in Underdeveloped Countries," p. 6. This thesis is most closely associated, however, with the name of Professor Paul N. Rosenstein-Rodan. He has stated it most fully and persuasively in his "Notes on the Theory of the 'Big Push,'" chap. iii of *Economic Development for Latin America: Proceedings of a Conference Held by the International Economic Association,* H. S. Ellis and H. W. Wallich (eds.) (London: Macmillan & Co., Ltd., 1961).

able group of individuals are exerting their energies imaginatively in technology, and if a large social overhead project is advantageous but not feasible, their energies will run to other small-scale improvements until, as income rises and the large-scale project becomes increasingly advantageous because of the increasing volume of activity, resources will be accumulated to carry it out, possibly with governmental support to mobilize the entire community's resources for the purpose.

Moreover, many transport and some types of power projects can in fact be built piecemeal. Roads can be and have been built or improved effectively by labor-intensive methods and a section at a time. So also have railroads, strange though this may seem to Americans. Again I cite the example of Colombia, where without exception railroads first appeared in stretches of a few miles out from the major cities, providing only local transportation within one valley.

Indeed, on cooler examination it appears that cases in which a lump of social overhead capital beyond the capacity of the economy to finance is of vital importance must be very rare indeed. The unique virtue of social overhead capital is supposed to be that it provides necessary facilities for other industries. On closer examination, this means only that the presence of social overhead capital will reduce the cost of production in the enterprises it serves. But so will the presence of those industries reduce the cost of production of the services of social overhead capital. The capital and service cost per vehicle using a modern road, if only a few vehicles per week do so, is enormous. In this respect the relationship between social overhead capital and other capital is symmetrical. Neither has a unique property. The special function of social overhead capital turns out to be largely an illusion.

No serious empirical evidence has been presented in print to support the social overhead capital hypothesis. The small amount of relevant research I have done contradicts it. In England, while the ocean always provided easy coastal transportation, the history of the eighteenth century gives no impression that construction of other social overhead capital preceded economic growth and permitted it. Rather, various types of investment proceeded *pari passu*. The construction of canals and roads within the country typically followed an increase in the demand for coal, timber, stone, and so on in urban centers. This demand of course is evidence of economic growth already proceeding. In turn, the roads and canals facilitated further progress.[4]

[4] For a moderately detailed study of economic growth during the century, see T. S. Ashton, *An Economic History of England: the 18th Century* (London: Methuen & Co., Ltd., 1955). Concerning transportation, see especially chap. iii.

A study of economic growth in Argentina likewise suggests that social overhead capital "grew *pari passu* with the economy as a whole rather than being laid down prior to development in other sectors."[5] This is certainly also true in Colombia, and I venture to suggest that it would be found true wherever detailed historical studies are made.[6]

THE THESIS OF THE NEED FOR A BIG PUSH

If it were true that income in underdeveloped societies is too low to permit saving and the market too small to justify investment, and in addition that large social overhead capital projects are a necessary base for technological progress, then it would follow that only a massive program to construct social overhead capital and to introduce income-raising projects all over the economy at once can get growth under way. To make this proposition consistent with the doctrine that income is too low to save, however, it must be held that the bar to saving is not physiological needs but rather merely a deep-seated unwillingness to save. Given this fact, and assuming that people may be aroused to a superhuman effort who would not be stirred to action by a smaller challenge, the thesis that a large comprehensive effort or "big push" is needed to start growth is internally consistent.

While the theory has been presented in an elaborate and attractive form by Harvey Leibenstein,[7] it was earlier advanced by Professor Rodan.[8] Professor Rodan presents it mainly as a prescription

[5] The quoted statements are from an unpublished study by Charles Cooper based primarily on an unpublished dissertation by Manual Zymelman, "The Economic History of Argentina, 1933–52," Massachusetts Institute of Technology, 1958. Within the social overhead capital category, railroad construction began in 1857 and bulked large from 1891 to 1914, and other types of social overhead capital formation replaced it later. However, much of the early railroad construction did not serve multiple industries, the classic function of social overhead capital, but tapped the grain lands of the interior and, as Cooper says, was "somewhat like spur tracks leading to a gold mine."

[6] It should be noted, however, that if the social overhead capital thesis is refined to the statement that in certain circumstances investment in social overhead capital will yield greater returns than other investment, and for various reasons merits special attention in government policy, then the statement is indisputable. R. S. Eckaus has noted in an unpublished study that a high rate of railroad investment in South Italy after the unification of North and South had relatively little effect on the rate of growth. See his "The Development of Regional Economic Differentials in Italy: North and South after Unification" (Cambridge: Center for International Studies, Massachusetts Institute of Technology, 1959).

[7] In his book, *Economic Backwardness and Economic Growth* (New York: John Wiley & Sons, Inc., 1957), chaps. viii and ix.

[8] See note 3 above.

for getting growth started rapidly at present rather than as an historical explanation of how growth started. His suggestion put the theory in the most attractive light. One may remark that if technological creativity is absent in the society, the big push will be impossible, whereas if technological creativity is present in considerable degree growth will start gradually without a big push, but in the latter situation a big push might accelerate it.

In any event, the theory of the big push does not explain why growth has begun in some societies and not in others, for historically the presence or absence of a big push is not the distinguishing feature. One may reasonably ask: Has growth anywhere started with a big push?

HOWARD S. ELLIS

"Big Push" Theories*

An important line of cleavage now exists between what may be called the "balanced growth" theories on the one hand, and the "big push" theories on the other. The former shows great affinity with the classical and neoclassical theories, stressing the maximizing of output by a "correct" allocation of factors so as to achieve equal marginal—or equal marginal social—product in all lines of activity. The other category ordinarily does not directly deny this line of thought, but chooses to lay greater emphasis in a dynamic setting upon other factors. Among these is the supposed necessity of a *large initial* increase in the rate of saving and investing, the feature which I characterize as the "big push."

Different writers invest this theory with varying nuances and meanings, but the present essay is less concerned with authors than with ideas. My interest attaches primarily to the *rationale* which has been offered in support of the "big push" theories of economic devel-

* From Howard S. Ellis, "'Big Push' Theories of Economic Development," *L'Industria* (Milan, 1957), pp. 3–12. Reprinted by permission of the author and of *L'Industria.*

opment, and the accompanying tendencies of these writers to emphasize the advantages of *state intervention* and of investment in *manufacturing,* as opposed to agriculture, extractive, and other industries.

Perhaps the commonest ground for the belief in a large initial burst of saving and investing engineered by the state is the advantages held forth by internal and external economies. Both rest upon discreteness or lumpiness in investment in particular capital goods. The other main arguments for a "critical minimum effort" or big push in investment rest upon certain lags in the *income-saving* nexus and in the relation of *population* growth to income.

1. INTERNAL AND EXTERNAL ECONOMIES

In consequence of technical indivisibilities, capital installations cannot always be made in small units. One version of the "big push" theory maintains that this fact makes necessary a large wave of investment in the initial phases of development. I do not feel that this idea is entirely to be discounted, but – given the fact of a minimum size of capital goods in certain industries – there are a number of reasons why the resulting wave in the *aggregate* demand for capital need not be large.

In the first place the wave would be considerably smoothed out by the differing lengths of construction periods for various types of investment goods and by an overlapping which would naturally occur through differing dates of origin, and which could easily be increased by some conscious control. Secondly, underdeveloped countries are generally advised, because of the scarcity of capital relatively to labor, to undertake investments which are not capital intensive; and so far as this advice is followed, the wave of demand for capital is lessened. Certain types of manufacturing, power production, chemical processes, and public utility installations are technologically possible only with large and intensive uses of capital, however, and something still remains to support the "big push" thesis.

But thirdly, in these very cases, we have typically to do with decreasing costs from internal economies, which conventional theory recognizes as a "naturally monopolistic" situation. Professor Stigler has argued that, because of the small size of domestic markets in underdeveloped countries, monopolies of this sort will be fairly numerous.[1] But to the same degree, unless monopoly profits are

[1] George J. Stigler, "The Division of Labor Is Limited by the Extent of the Market," *Journal of Political Economy,* June 1951, pp. 185–193.

entirely eliminated by state control, there would be an especially strong inducement for capital supply to match the strong demand.

Fourthly, in so far as the market is not limited to domestic sales or, if thus limited, represents a substitution of domestic markets for imports, a technically fixed minimum investment need not be large relatively to aggregate demand, and the overhead charge per unit of output for interest and amortization need not be formidable.

The weight of these offsets to technical discreteness as a reason for a necessary wave of investment, or to the difficulty of managing it where it is present, varies in importance from one country to another. But in many under-developed economies the most pressing types of investment are small scale improvements in agriculture, in agricultural processing, in small scale industry, and in some types of public works such as highways, drainage, irrigation, sanitary installation, schools, and the like, which can often be constructed in small stages without capital intensive techniques. In these cases, the problem of technical discreteness does not even arise, and internal economies are unimportant.

Some external economies, aside from those of a "pecuniary" sort,[2] are internal economies at one remove (or more) from the original industry; much the same considerations are relevant. Viner has presented an evaluation of external economies to which not much can be added.[3] Expansion of output may yield not only economies but diseconomies through the force of diminishing returns, and the net outcome depends on the balance of two forces. Where the net balance *appears* to be favorable and comes from the imposition of protective tariffs or granting of subsidies, it has to be considered whether the industries "taxed" (directly or by reduced domestic demand in consequence of taxes on consumers) would not have realized economies in absence of these burdens.

While Viner's argument is oriented to the pro's and con's of protective tariffs in order to achieve external economies, it is also

[2] Pecuniary external economies, such as the advantages of buying or selling in large lots, are in large measure (though not exclusively) gains of one firm or industry or group of consumers from another economic unit, and hence are not net national gains, unless the items enter into exports or imports. Even there, considering the usual scale of these operations relatively to the world market, not much can be expected from increased volume of sales. Consequently in the present discussion pecuniary external economies need not be given significant weight.

[3] Jacob Viner, "Stability and Progress: the Poorer Countries' Problem," International Economic Association, First Congress, Rome, September 6–11, 1956, mimeographed paper, pp. 27–31.

directly applicable to the pro's and con's of a large wave of investment for the same purpose. Any external economies which might be achievable through an expansion of exports depend upon the world market for exports and not upon the volume of domestic investment. Similarly, investment for the production of import substitutes would be incapable of achieving external economies in excess of those already secured by the previous imports, which also have been produced for the much larger world market. Furthermore, in the same measure as investment is cost-reducing but not output-expanding, the whole argument for external economies falls away. As Viner correctly points out, a very large part of investment in underdeveloped countries is undertaken for exports, import substitutes, and for cost reduction; consequently the importance of the "big push" of investment to achieve external economies is probably small.

To Viner's argument it is only necessary to add that for investment *not* oriented to export, import substitutes, and to cost reduction without output expansion (that is, for domestic consumption not substituting for imports and for cost reduction *cum* output expansion) the qualifications of the preceding section relative to gains from *internal* economies also apply to *external* economies, because external economies are internal at one remove. Compounding Viner's with these qualifications results in a small probability of gain in external economies from a large wave of investment. External economies there are, indeed, but they come partly from international trade in proportion to its volume, and partly from the ordinary course of and in proportion to domestic economic development, without much dependence upon a *wave* of investment.

2. THE RELATION OF SAVING TO INCOME

In the thinking of a number of advocates of the big push, an important role is played by the possibility of a lag of consumption behind a sudden increase of per capita income. If investment can be pushed fast by foreign capital or various sources of domestic compulsory saving, the lag of consumption produces a wave of voluntary saving from domestic incomes and thus helps to set the economy on the way toward development.

But a number of reasons exist for doubting whether this lag in consumption affords a particularly important justification of an "all-out" investment effort. In the first place, the theory assumes that the basic difficulty is a low ratio of savings to income. While this assumption is probably correct for most economies on a very low level of per capita incomes, it is not universally true. Peter Bauer has assembled evidence that saving in private agriculture and trade in Nigeria and other underdeveloped countries is substantial and considerably exceeds official estimates.[4] Furthermore, because a great deal of saving in primitive economies may go into unproductive forms, such as doweries, ceremonial observances, churches and temples, and hoards of money, precious metals or gems, the fact that there has been saving may elude the observer. But this reflection also points to another weakness of the lag of consumption argument. The gain is essentially temporary so far as concerns the ratio of saving to income: after the posited spurt of investment and per capita incomes, the economy falls back into its old habits of improvidence or unproductive use of savings. While the capital accumulated during the spurt may, *if maintained*, yield somewhat higher incomes, this qualification is also important, and the net gain may be problematical.

Furthermore, as a subsequent analysis will emphasize, the spurt of economic improvement may first lower the death rate and thus increase population so rapidly that per capita incomes do not rise. In this event the lag thesis regarding consumption is irrelevant. A further restriction upon the sphere of applicability of the consumption lag is that it relies upon some *deus ex machina* to supply the wave of investment — upon foreign capital or domestic forced saving — so that at best its role is merely supplementary.

Indeed many of the advocates of the "critical minimum effort" thesis do not rely upon a lag of consumption at all. The possibility of rapid increases in population, the demands for wage increases and extended social security, the tendency of governments to demonstrate their "democratic" character or the prowess of their country relatively to richer nations by lavish outlays, the so-called "demonstration effect" of foreign consumption habits, and finally the possible adverse reaction of private voluntary saving to various forms of enforced frugality — all of these would lead to a considerable degree of scepticism as to the possibility of much of an increase in saving as a lag phenomenon, even where per capita incomes increase.

3. THE RELATION OF POPULATION TO INCOME

A second type of lag which plays a role in "big push" theorizing is the idea that if *per capita* incomes can be raised rapidly, the popula-

[4] Peter Bauer, Gonville and Caius College, Cambridge: *The Underdeveloped Economies: a Critique of Current Ideas,* mimeographed, 1956.

tion will protect its newly achieved welfare by family limitation. Reversing the implication of Malthus' revised doctrine of population, according to which the "preventive checks" were the means of achieving a higher real income (the *standard* of living *determines* the level of living), this line of thought reverses the causation: the lower birthrate is induced by higher incomes.

The difficulty here is the slowness of the operation of this factor. As Lewis says, "If raising the standard of living is a necessary condition for bringing the birthrate down, it looks as if the population problem will be with us for a good long time yet."[5] It required something like two centuries of economic progress in England for the *per capita* income of the lower income groups, which supply most of the births, to fall appreciably.

Unfortunately the matter is even worse, as Notestein, among numbers of others, show. "The more rapid reduction of mortality than of fertility to the forces of modernization is probably inevitable. The reduction of mortality is a universally acceptable goal and faces no substantial social obstacles. But the reduction of fertility requires a shift of social goals. . . . This change . . . is at best a slow process. As a result, the period of modernization is virtually certain to yield rapid population increase."[6] In view of these facts it would seem difficult if not impossible to hope to alleviate population pressure by a "big push" on investment and output.

Coupling a conviction similar to Notestein's that mortality would fall faster than the decline of the birthrate with the conclusion of Section II (above) that consumption would rise as fast as per capita incomes, Galenson and Leibenstein rely essentially upon a big wave of investment and forced saving by the State; only eventually would increased output accrue to gains in *per capita* consumption.[7] If increased productivity and production are ploughed back into investment goods, standards (or more accurately, levels) of living cannot rise and thus the rise of the birthrate, which these authors fear in consequence of larger incomes, cannot occur. Only eventually and with an undetermined lag can the increase of national income be allowed to flow into consumption.

[5] W. Arthur Lewis, *The Theory of Economic Growth*, London, 1955, p. 315.

[6] Frank W. Notestein, "Population – The Long View" in Theodore W. Schultz (ed.), *Food for the World*, pp. 40–41; quoted by Galenson and Leibenstein, in the publication cited below, p. 364.

[7] Walter Galenson and Harvey Leibenstein, "Investment Criteria, Productivity, and Economic Development," *Quarterly Journal of Economics*, Vol. LXIX, August 1955, pp. 343–370, cf. also Harvey Leibenstein, *A Theory of Economic-Demographic Development*, Princeton University Press, 1954, Ch. IV–V.

This prescription is somewhat veiled by other parts of a rather complex theory and by technical language. Galenson and Leibenstein would abandon "marginal productivity in the usual sense" as the criterion for the allocation of investment; instead they adopt the "marginal per capita reinvestment quotient." This signifies the application of techniques which "lead ultimately to the maximum capital/labor ratio." They do not indicate when this maximizing of the capital/labor ratio is to be abandoned in favor of something more favorable to the consumer, but continually emphasize that "the greater the gap between output and consumption, the less the rate of population growth and the less the dilution of capital." (e.g., p. 352)

Other parts of the theory involve the adoption of techniques indicated by the "marginal per capita reinvestment quotient," even if they are labor-saving in a surplus-labor economy, and the use of long-lived capital goods, even if capital is relatively scarce, provided the technique conforms to the criterion proposed. They favor types of investment holding forth promise of external economies, the most modern and efficient techniques for their power to break through traditionalism, and industrial – as opposed to agricultural – forms of investment because it encourages the growth of cities and a population characterized by lower birthrates than that of rural areas.

The model of Galenson and Leibenstein is not devoid, I believe, of important suggestions for the evolution of a satisfactory theory of development; but so far as concerns their version of the "critical minimum effort," a number of over-riding objections appear. In the first place, the criterion for investment according to the "marginal reinvestment quotient" is a technical phrase which thinly veils the harsh prescription that the State plough back all productivity gains into "investment for further re-investment," and the ethics of this prescription may be challenged. There is a vast difference between this and the democratic determination of saving ratios, either through individual free choice in a price economy, or through legislative choice via taxation in a free economy. In the second place one may legitimately question whether this extreme (and totalitarian) sort of procedure could long endure in anything approaching a regime of popular government. Galenson and Leibenstein themselves observe that "the process of development must be sufficiently rapid to satisfy the swiftly burgeoning aspiration of people suddenly released from a Malthusian world and endowed with political power." (op. cit., p. 369) Can one readily imagine that these "burgeoning aspirations" can be satisfied merely by the growth of productive capacity, with no increase in the *per capita* level of consumption?

These misgivings pertain to the social ethics and the political practicability of the "big push." But more significant still is the weakness in the analytical model itself, which must *finally* rely upon voluntary family limitation when — at long last — the big push is past history and the increase of the productive apparatus is allowed to accrue to increases of per capita consumption. Aside from the suggestion that the "marginal re-investment quotient" involves a certain (query: how great?) favoring of industry in order to induce the growth of cities and reduce average fecundity, these authors are still vulnerable to their own misgiving that rising *per capita* incomes will simply produce a rise in the birthrate. If so, an *induced* rise of the standard of living simply through a higher level of living must be abandoned — or at least not trusted very far — as a means of preventing a population explosion. The emphasis would have to be laid upon *direct* means such as the "shift of social goals" which Notestein emphasizes, through improvement in the social status of women, in literacy, and in knowledge and availability of birth control methods, and the like, all of which have secondary or no relation to a burst of enforced saving and investment.

4. INDUSTRIALIZATION AND DEVELOPMENT

Theorists who hold that a sudden thrust of investment and output is necessary to engender economic growth will generally be found adhering to the idea that manufacturing industry makes a quite special contribution to development. This association is, of course, not accidental. In the first place, manufacturing would be expected to show more numerous instances of large indivisible capital units than would agriculture, trade, and service industries. Second, from the demographic angle, urban life is supposed to contribute toward reduced fertility. And third, for those who stress the "critical minimum effort" and the desirability of introducing labor-saving techniques in order to maximize output, industry may seem to hold forth more opportunities of this sort.

None of these supposed grounds for favoring industry, however, will survive inspection. If the argument of a previous section is valid — granting that manufacturing more frequently displays "lumpiness" in capital units than other industries — internal and external economies can be realized without a spurt in aggregate saving and investment to the degree that industries overlap in their gestation periods by virtue of differing lengths of these periods or scattering in the dates of initiation. But even if this evening up of the flow of demand is not complete, internal and external economies resulting from investment in plants producing exports and import substitutes, and in those cases where investment reduces costs without expanding output do not depend upon an expansion of the domestic market. Thus the case for a spurt of investment in order to capture internal and external economies is attenuated practically to the vanishing point, and with it also any special advantage in industrial over other forms of investment.

The second line of argument may indeed afford some grounds for preferring the development of industry, *if* urbanization actually proves in the given instance to lower fertility rates, *if* the social and economic costs of cities do not appear to be an excessive price for this gain, and *if* – perhaps most importantly – direct means of reducing the birthrate through education, improvements in the status of women, and the dissemination of birth-control methods appear to be more costly or less available than building cities for their indirect effect on fertility! Even so, however, I am not aware that this effect is coupled, even in the minds of the writers treated in these pages, with a big push of savings and investment in industry. A given amount evenly distributed through time should have approximately the same effects on urbanization and fertility: indeed, the effects, by avoiding slums and inadequate public facilities, should be even more beneficial.

Perhaps the most difficult argument to justify in support of a generally superior role of manufacturing industry in economic development is that which apparently is thought to follow from the idea of a "critical minimum effort." Cases may indeed exist, as Galenson and Leibenstein argue, where "increasing the amount of excess labor by the introduction of labor-displacing capital can result in a greater addition to output than the use of labor-absorbing capital."[8] What is the evidence, however, that such cases might not be as frequently encountered in agriculture as in manufacturing?

An equally pertinent question is, what becomes of the new increment to unemployed persons? Galenson and Leibenstein's argument would be conclusive if the only issue were productive efficiency. If labor in agriculture exists in surplus, i.e. if marginal productivity, while not necessarily zero is nevertheless less than subsistence, the margin between actual marginal product and subsistence must be borne out of the product of infra-marginal laborers. It can, of course be argued that if the labor-saving technique is more productive, the

[8] Galenson and Leibenstein, *op. cit.*, p. 349; hyphens not in original.

aggregate output available for supporting all laborers (employed plus unemployed) is larger and therefore the problem is easier. But institutionally the added output may not accrue to the same units as become responsible for the support of the newly unemployed, and thus their burden may become intolerable. Finally it may be recalled that in the model of these two writers, the added product does not become available for consumption expenditure at all, but is instead channeled completely into expanding plant.

In retrospect, no general presumption favorable to the allocation of investment to industry is established by the big push doctrines. In fact, for most of the low-income underdeveloped regions of the world, the general presumption – which of course can be outweighed in particular cases by special conditions – is all the other way. Agriculture makes relatively light drafts upon high technical skills, upon entrepreneurial abilities, and upon capital, all of which are generally scarce in these regions. New techniques can frequently be introduced without much expense. Surplus agricultural labor can be turned into a source of economic development in village and other local undertakings and in processing agricultural products *in situ* and without the economic costs and social disruptions of transplanting the labor to cities. But most important is the fact that most underdeveloped countries now earn their livelihood in primary production and must set out on the road to economic development with the resources they already have available.

5. ECONOMIC PROGRESS AND GOVERNMENT

The allocation of investment so as to achieve equal marginal products in all lines is the essence of economics, and the "balanced growth" theory of economic development is little more than a re-assertion of this optimum in a dynamic setting. This holds true whether the principle is couched in older-fashioned terms such as marginal productivity, or in newer terms such as marginal social productivity or allocation through linear programming.

Any intelligent application of marginal analysis to a developing economy must take into consideration the fact that what may not be advisable in the short run may be the superior route for the long run. Thus the classical theory of international trade has always admitted the possible gains of infant industry protection; and liberal economists have never denied that temporary monoply, through charters, patents, and copyrights, may conduce to long-run growth. But the exception proves the rule. The conclusion of infant industry protection is not that the less the volume of exports and imports the better; and the conclusion of patent concessions is not that universal monopoly is superior to competition.

The marginal principle, save perhaps in the case of consumer free choice of expenditure, is *per se* neutral with respect to the merits of private versus State enterprise. To some economists, the realization of equal marginal productivity in all lines of production has presented a case for authoritarian planning. But as Albert Hirschman has pointed out, it is simply impossible to carry the art of statistical projection to the refined point of balancing marginal product in all possible uses. What the economist can do is help in the cost versus returns assessment of a specific project here and there which holds forth considerable promise.[9] In like vein, Paul Streeten writes, "If the economist is to give advice in concrete situations, it is more helpful for him to think in terms of *improvements* than in terms of ideals or optima."[10] The value of the optimum through marginal equalization lies perhaps more in a warning of disproportional development than in a precise indication of just what and how much to produce. State planning certainly receives no especial benediction from the marginal principle.

"Big push" economists are generally strong interventionists, as even a casual inspection of the writers referred to at the outset will reveal. To harvest external economies, to overcome technological lumpiness, to induce saving or lower birthrates they favor the forced draft of infant industry protection, or inflation, or appropriation of the agricultural surplus, or state control of investment, or exchange control, or some combination of these, including various hues of planning, socialism, and communism.

Anything approaching an adequate treatment of the title of this section would require a book and another author. But something useful on the subject may be won from the foregoing pages. No one of the discontinuities and lags analyzed here offers convincing evidence of significant gains normally to be expected as by-products of engineering a concentration of investment and rate of increase of output for an initial upward burst.

If the rate of progress can be sustained, and if speed does not

[9] Albert O. Hirschman, "Economics and Investment Planning: Reflections Based on Experience in Colombia," in *Investment Criteria and Economic Growth,* mimeographed, Center for International Studies, M.I.T., Cambridge, Mass., 1955.

[10] Paul Streeten, "Programs and Prognoses," *Quarterly Journal of Economics,* August 1954, pp. 355–376; see p. 367, italics in original.

prove to be its own undoing through misapplication of capital, inflations, balance of payments troubles, capital flights, and the like, then of course a big push to development is better than a small one. In the development episodes of the past, the economic historians, such as Cairncross and Gerschenkron, and the economic theorists, such as Spiethoff and Schumpeter have laid great weight upon entrepreneurial innovation, upon the initiating role of migration and of direct capital investment, and the influence of the trader. It does not seem to be given that the interventions of the state in the form of tariffs, exchange controls, regulation of investment, and the like must deliver the thrust. Countries characterized as underdeveloped economically are frequently also underdeveloped politically; their citizens often expect of these governments economic attainments far beyond their capacity.[11] It would not, I believe, be a particularly difficult task to show that the economic development of many Latin American countries in recent years has taken place despite, rather than because of, the activities of governments. Ordinary economic motivations of the individual and firm are a powerful engine of economic progress. It would be regrettable if the economists of the free world created an impression to the contrary.

HLA MYINT

Big Push and Balanced Growth*

Hla Myint outlines a theory of low income trap which assumes that small increases in investment and per capita income induce population growth which nullifies the increase in per capita income. He questions the assumptions of this theory and its policy implications that an under-

[11] Richard F. Behrendt, "Eine Freiheitliche Entwicklungspolitik für Materiell Zurückgebliebene Länder," *Ordo*, Vol. 8, 1956, pp. 67–122.

* From Hla Myint, *The Economics of the Developing Countries*, pp. 117–127. Reprinted by permission of Hutchinson Publishing Group Ltd. and of Frederick A. Praeger, Inc., publishers of the American edition.

developed country must undertake a "critical minimum effort" in investment to produce a faster rate of growth of income than the maximum possible rate of growth of population (between 3 and 4 percent per year). Myint then outlines and questions two versions of the Balanced Growth (BG) theory.

The first version of BG, as expounded by P. N. Rosenstein-Rodan, assumes the existence of adequate social overhead capital and investible resources and advocates the need for simultaneous expansion of consumer goods industries to create interdependent demands for the new supplies of goods. The second version of BG advocates the necessity of investing in social overhead capital as well as in many industries simultaneously for new factories to succeed.

Myint points out that the capital requirements for industrialization implicit in the second approach are greater than in the first and still greater in the third version of BG (reproduced below). He argues that these versions of BG and their conclusions rest on questionable assumptions and reasoning: thus technological lumpiness of social overhead capital need not mean economic lumpiness of investment, nor are price and income elasticities of demand and substitution possibilities between new and old consumer goods so low or markets so small in poor countries as to dictate that one new enterprise cannot find adequate markets for its products. The "all or nothing" approach implied in these versions of Balanced Growth, in Myint's judgment, is unwarranted.

THE third version of the balanced growth theory, the "big push," is nothing short of an attempt to introduce a comprehensive and integrated programme of industrialization, including within its framework not only the consumers' goods industries and social overhead investment but also capital goods industries. The only thing left out here seems to be the agricultural sector. It is argued that in order to launch economic development successfully, it is necessary not only to enlarge the size of the market and obtain "internal economies" of large-scale production, but also to obtain the "external economies" which arise from simultaneously setting up industries which are technically interdependent with each other; that while these "technical complementarities" do not normally exist between a horizontal group of consumers' goods industries at the same stage of production, they are very important between a vertical group of industries at different stages of production; and that since these external economies are particularly important in the capital goods industries which supply each other and the consumers' goods industries with various inputs in the form of machinery and semi-processed intermediate goods, the capital goods sector should form an integral part of the balanced growth programme. This comprehensive version of the theory therefore tries to fulfil simultaneously three sets of balanced growth relations: (i) the horizontal balance between different consumers' goods industries determined by the pattern of expansion in consumers' demand; (ii) the balance between social overhead investment and the directly productive activities both in the consumers' and the capital goods sectors; and (iii) the vertical balance between the capital goods industries, including the intermediate goods and the consumers' goods industries, determined by the technical complementarities.

Two main features stand out in this version (c) of the theory. The first is the "external economies" argument: in pursuing this we shall be led to some of the issues involved in the question of the relative importance of planning and free enterprise in promoting economic development in the underdeveloped countries. The second is the argument for comprehensive programming which has been likened to an attempt to impose a complete and brand new "second floor" on the weak and imperfectly developed one-floor economy of these countries. In examining this argument for comprehensiveness, we shall see the basic weakness of the all-or-nothing approach which is more pronounced in version (c) than in the previous versions.

In welfare economics, "external economies" are defined as unpaid services which accrue to third parties. These are not fully reflected in private costs and products so that the market prices have to be corrected to take them into account. In the development literature, the concept is used in a different sense. The "external economies" are the "pecuniary" economies transmitted through the price system. They originate in a given industry A (say due to the internal economies of overcoming technical indivisibilities) and are then passed on in the form of a lower price for A's product to another industry B which uses it as an input or a factor of production. New investment in A which overcomes its technical indivisibilities will cheapen its product. "The profits of industry B created by the lower price of factor A, call for investment and expansion in industry B, one result of which will be an increase in industry B's demand for industry A's product. This in its turn will give rise to profits and call for further investment and expansion of industry A."[1]

Now it is argued that this mutually beneficial type of expansion in output will not take place to the fullest possible extent without a balanced growth planning. This is so, first, because of the inadequacy of free market prices to act as a signalling device informing private investors about *future* possibilities of expansion in the complementary industries A and B; and secondly because of the imperfect response of private enterprise in the underdeveloped countries to a given signal from the price system. In order to reap the "external economies" to the full extent, the investment in the two complementary industries would have to be planned together and carried out in an integrated way by a planning authority.

It is true that with an embryonic or imperfectly developed capital market and "futures" market, the price mechanism in most underdeveloped countries is a very poor signalling system, particularly about future events. But on the other hand, the institutional and administrative machinery available for the governments of the underdeveloped countries is also, with a few exceptions, notoriously weak. It is difficult, therefore, to generalize whether the communication system about future events will always improve with a greater degree of state planning, without taking into account the particular circumstances of each case.

The general problems of co-ordinating a complex integrated development plan of the type required by version (c) of the balanced growth theory are well known, and they are frequently thought to be beyond the competence even of the stronger and more efficient governmental machinery of the advanced countries. Two points may however be emphasized. First, the governments of the underdeveloped countries are likely to face their greatest difficulties, not in the initial drawing up of the economic development plans (frequently done with the assistance of foreign experts), but in the execution of the various projects according to a planned time-table and in keeping the different departments and agencies *continually informed* about progress in carrying out the plans. In carrying out a complex set of related projects, there are bound to be various revisions of the original plans, delays and departures from the original timetable. The greater the interdependence between the different components of the plan, the greater the repercussions of an unexpected

[1] T. Scitovsky, "Two Concepts of External Economies," *Journal of Political Economy,* April 1954.

or unavoidable change in one part of the plan on the rest, and the greater the need to keep the different parts of the plans continually revised in the light of latest available information. These problems of co-ordination, even within the different parts of the public sector, are formidable, and it is not surprising if "progress reporting" remains one of the weakest parts of the planning machinery. Secondly, one of the most serious gaps in knowledge required for planning is likely to arise, not merely from a lack of general "technical know-how" but from ignorance of the local conditions in the underdeveloped countries themselves, and inefficient "feedback" of this vital local knowledge from the different parts of the country to the central planning machinery. Nor can this be easily remedied, as is commonly supposed, by improving the standard type of statistical information. Frequently local information relevant for efficient planning depends on the qualitative differences and local peculiarities which are abstracted from the statistical compilations concerned with obtaining comparable sets of figures for the country as a whole.

So far we have been concerned with the problems of co-ordination between the different parts of the government sector. But most underdeveloped countries have a considerable private sector in agriculture and consumers' goods industries, traditional and modern; and some countries like India have an important private sector even in the capital goods industries. Thus, in order to assess a comprehensive balanced growth programme, we have to take into account the rather neglected problem of economic development in the "mixed economy," viz. the problem of co-ordination between the government and the private sector. The problem is simpler when the two sectors are complementary; for instance, the government may inform the private sector about its future plans to expand transport and communications or power and may expect the private sector to embark on complementary investment (even here uncertainties about time-tables for the completion of government projects can create difficulties). The problem of co-ordination and communication becomes formidable when the two sectors are competitive, say either because the government is planning to set up factories to compete with private firms in a given industry or threatening to nationalize private competitors, or because both the government and the private sector are competing for some scarce resources, normally the limited foreign exchange reserves of the country. In this situation, a "cold war" has developed between the two sectors in many underdeveloped countries. The government departments tend to keep their plans and intentions secret from the private businessmen because they fear "speculative" activities which will disrupt their plans. On the other hand, private enterprise is inhibited by uncertainties not only about the general economic situation but also about the future intentions of the government and future changes in government regulations. These uncertainties are aggravated when the government, with its drive for a large-scale development plan straining its resources, gets itself into a "crisis" situation where it is obliged to resort to sudden tightening of controls, notably foreign exchange controls, which upset not only its own plans but also those of the private sector.

Thus, it seems too optimistic to hope that the adoption of comprehensive balanced-growth investment planning by itself, without fundamental improvements in the administrative machinery of the government, and the easing of mutual distrust and suspicion between the government and the private sectors, would improve the efficiency of signalling and co-ordination between the different sectors of the economy.

Let us now pass on to the question of the responsiveness of private enterprise in underdeveloped countries to a given signal from the price system. Logically, the fact that two industries A and B are complementary does not necessarily mean that they should be expanded simultaneously to reach the maximum possible expansion for both. With the responsiveness of private enterprise, this expansion may be achieved either by expanding A to the full extent and inducing B to expand correspondingly by lowering the price of the input A, or by expanding B to the full extent, inducing A to expand correspondingly under the pressure of excess demand for its product by B. In the advanced countries, this may take place through private initiative only, resulting in what is known as "vertical integration." Even in the underdeveloped countries, the state may need to expand through its own initiative either A or B only, rather than both as suggested by the balanced growth theory.

Stressing this possibility, Professor Hirschman has built up an alternative strategy of economic development: the deliberately "unbalanced growth" approach.[2] He agrees with the balanced growth theorists about the importance of technical complementarities between industries at different stages of production which he calls "vertical linkages," but arrives at the opposite conclusion by introducing two further propositions.

First, he points out that the degree of complementarity is stronger between some particular groups of industries than others.

[2] A. O. Hirschman, *The Strategy of Economic Development*, Chs. 3–6.

Thus the aim of development policy should be not to push forward simultaneously on all fronts as though these complementarities were uniformly distributed all over the economy, but to select and concentrate on particular "strategic" sectors of the economy where these interdependent linkage effects may be expected to be strongest. He believes that these strategic parts of the economy are to be found where the network of input-output relationships is thickest, representing industries which buy the largest part of their inputs from other industries, or sell the largest part of their outputs to other industries (as distinct from the final consumers), or both.

Secondly, he argues that the balanced growth approach, even if it were successful, will merely achieve a once-for-all increase in national income, coming to rest at a higher plateau representing the balanced growth equilibrium. Economic development, however, should be a continuous dynamic process, kept alive by the tensions of shortages and excess supplies and by the disequilibria in the strategic sectors which are capable of responding to these pace-setting pressures. The balanced growth theorists would like the two complementary industries A and B to expand simultaneously to their "full" equilibrium level which would exhaust the external economies possible in the initial situation. Professor Hirschman would like either A or B to overshoot the equilibrium point. He hopes that the resulting pressures of excess demand or excess supply would change the initial situation itself and lead to further economic developments in a series of "leap-frogging" movements.

The whole question depends to a large extent on the assumption we make about the responsiveness of private enterprise in the underdeveloped countries to a disequilibrium situation with profitable opportunities of increasing investment. The balanced growth theorists are thinking of a situation where the complementary industries are new industries requiring a considerable initial outlay of capital and technical experience on the part of the new entrants into them. They feel that it is beyond the capacity of unaided private enterprise in the underdeveloped countries to respond effectively to this situation so that the government must take the initiative in launching a balanced growth programme. There are, however, considerable differences among the balanced growth theorists themselves over the question how much of the programme should be directly carried by the government planning authority. Some are content merely to point out the theoretical advantages of the balanced growth approach without specifying the exact proportion of the "mixed economy." Others are contemptuous about "patching up the market" and imply that the bulk of the balanced growth programme, not only in the social overhead capital but also in the capital and the consumers' goods sectors, should be carried out by state enterprise.

The popular argument concerning the shortage of entrepreneurs in the underdeveloped countries, however, is not a sufficient reason for increasing the government sector. For if the private sector suffers from a shortage of entrepreneurs, the government sector will equally suffer from a shortage of administrators who can perform these entrepreneurial functions. As Professor Hirschman has pointed out, the balanced growth approach makes an impossible demand on the underdeveloped countries by requiring them to provide, all at once, entrepreneurs and managers to run a whole flock of new industries; if they could do this, they would not be underdeveloped in the first place. But he believes that the problem of increasing the supply of entrepreneurs and capital can be solved in the long run, provided the right type of pressures are used to bring them forth. He believes that, if suitable investment opportunities are opened up by his unbalanced growth approach, additional supplies of domestic savings will be forthcoming, and that what is holding back many underdeveloped countries is not so much the shortage of savings as the "ability to invest." Similarly, the unbalanced growth approach may be regarded as providing a school for entrepreneurs, spelling out their profit opportunities in block letters by means of deliberately engineered bottlenecks and excess capacities, and thus assisting the "learning process" of the potential entrepreneurs in the underdeveloped countries.

Other aspects of the controversy between the balanced growth and the unbalanced growth approaches will be considered in Chapters 9 and 10. For the moment, I shall conclude this chapter by pointing out the basic weakness of the all-or-nothing approach which version (c) of the balanced growth theory suffers from more than the previous versions. The crucial practical question which faces the developing countries is not how to plan their development programmes as though they had unlimited supplies of resources, but what sort of choices they should make when their currently available resources are insufficient for a comprehensive balanced growth programme. The question of having to make unpalatable choices has been pushed into the background, first by the assumption of the "unlimited supply of labour" and second by the expectation of greater foreign aid. In the previous chapter, we have already seen that the cushion provided by the economic potential from "disguised unemployment" is very thin. So now the main reliance has to be placed on greater foreign aid. But however generous the supply of foreign aid, it can only relieve the harshness of choices rather than abolish the basic economic problem of having to make choices. This is particularly true when it is remembered that in many underdeveloped countries the basic "scarce factor" may not be the shortage of saving but the ability to absorb and invest capital effectively. It is the basic weakness of the various versions of the balanced growth theories that they obscure this problem of choice. The more comprehensive the minimum size of the development programme they advocate, the more the problem of choice is obscured.

For instance, the version (a) obscures the choices within the consumers' goods sector, but at an overall level the choice it makes is clear. If the underdeveloped countries do not have enough resources to push ahead on all fronts, they should concentrate on investment in consumers' goods industries, assuming the necessary capital goods can be imported through trade or aid. This choice is made on the basis that the limitation in the size of the market is the most important obstacle to economic development, and that the existing levels of consumption are so low that it is better to try to raise consumption immediately even at the cost of a slower rate of economic growth in the future. The converse of version (a), the "communist model" of industrialization, also makes a clear-cut choice, in favour of the capital goods sector. This is done presumably on the basis that the most important requirement for economic development is to be able to reap the technical economies of scale and complementarities, and that since these are most abundant in the capital goods sector, it is better to sacrifice present consumption for the sake of the faster rate of future economic growth. The "big push" or the version (c) of the balanced growth theory, however, insists on expanding investment, not only in the consumer's goods industries, but in the capital goods industries and also in the public utilities and social overhead capital. By insisting on this simultaneous expansion on all fronts, it has not only evaded the crucial economic choices between present and future income, but has frequently encouraged many underdeveloped countries to push too far beyond their currently available resources and organizing ability. This is frequently defended on the grounds that it might elicit more foreign aid. It is questionable, however, whether the prospect of foreign aid, which is far from certain, is sufficient to justify pushing the developing countries into a "crisis" situation in which they are no longer in a position to make any coherent or consistent choices and are merely driven from one ad hoc emergency measure to another. This is surely the reverse of "economic planning."

ALBERT O. HIRSCHMAN

Unbalanced Growth: An Espousal*

CLASSICAL economies, while not taking so positive a view of the imbalances of the growth process, at least was never particularly concerned about them because it relied on prices to signal, and on the profit motive to eliminate rapidly and reliably, any structural disequilibria that might arise in the course of growth. The critics of classical economics, on the other hand, have always pointed to cases in which these "market forces" would not act with adequate strength and speed. Having thus convinced themselves that the adjustment mechanism is beset with virtually insuperable obstacles, some of the critics naturally enough took the defeatist view that growth has to be balanced from the start or cannot take place at all.

This counsel of perfection is not only impractical but also uneconomical. We need not sacrifice the valuable development mechanisms brought into play by unbalanced growth, especially if we go beyond the overly narrow view of the adjustment process that has long dominated economic literature.

Tradition seems to require that economists argue forever about the question whether, in any disequilibrium situation, *market forces acting alone* are likely to restore equilibrium. Now this is certainly an interesting question. But as social scientists we surely must address ourselves also to the broader question: is the disequilibrium situation likely to be corrected at all, by market or nonmarket forces, or by both acting jointly? *It is our contention that nonmarket forces are not necessarily less "automatic" than market forces.* Certainly the almost monotonous regularity with which interventionist economists have come forward—and with which authorities have acted—when the market forces did not adequately perform their task testifies to the fact that we do not have to rely exclusively on price signals and profit-maximizers to save us from trouble.

The case of unbalanced growth provides a good illustration. When supply difficulties arise in the course of uneven progress in

* From Albert O. Hirschman, *The Strategy of Economic Development* (New Haven, 1958), pp. 63–65. Reprinted by permission of Yale University Press.

sectors—such as education and public utilities—where private enterprise is not operating, strong pressures are felt by public authorities to "do something"; and since the desire for political survival is at least as strong a motive force as the desire to realize a profit, we may ordinarily expect some corrective action to be taken.

There is no implication here that any disequilibrium whatsoever will be resolved by some combination of market and nonmarket forces. But if a community cannot generate the "induced" decisions and actions needed to deal with the supply disequilibria that arise in the course of uneven growth, then I can see little reason for believing that it will be able to take the set of "autonomous" decisions required by balanced growth. In other words, if the adjustment mechanism breaks down altogether, this is a sign that the community rejects economic growth as an overriding objective.

The inclusion of probable reactions of nonmarket forces not only serves to make economic analysis more realistic. It also protects us against a fallacious chain of reasoning that is fairly common in developing economics and of which the doctrine of balanced growth is itself an excellent illustration. In this reasoning, one first selects some objective of economic policy that seems desirable enough; then one proves that the objective cannot be attained through the operation of market forces; and one concludes that state action surely will bring the objective about. But this conclusion is clearly a non sequitur. The fact that private entrepreneurs will be unable or unwilling to do certain jobs which we would like to see done does not in itself ensure that the government can handle them. We must examine whether these jobs are likely to be performed satisfactorily by public authorities, which function after all in the same society as the entrepreneurs.

HANS W. SINGER

A Balanced View of Balanced Growth*

IN THE preceding section [of Singer's book], the doctrine of balanced growth has been offered on the one hand as a possible solution and one with some educational merit for underdeveloped countries, but on the other hand as an incomplete, implausible, and even potentially dangerous solution. Perhaps it is well now to amplify this judgment by standing back and taking a broader view of the problems involved. For this purpose, the elementary sketch of an underdeveloped economy may be re-introduced. There are several distinct roads to economic growth.

1) In the first place and most obviously, there is the increase in productivity in agriculture. It is not unnatural that foreign missions to underdeveloped countries should emphasize this road to economic growth: any visitor to an underdeveloped country will observe, first, that the bulk of the population – about 80 per cent in our sketch – is employed in agriculture; and, second, that agriculture is carried on at a particularly low level of productivity, not only in relation to agriculture in more advanced countries, but also in relation to other occupations in the same underdeveloped country. Higher productivity in agriculture must certainly be one of the main roads to economic growth. When it occurs it would normally solve the marketing difficulty; the higher incomes of farmers will provide expanded markets for industries and, according to Engel's Law, part of the additional demand is likely to be for nonagricultural products. Note, however, that the solution of the marketing difficulty through higher agricultural productivity is by no means automatic: where the higher productivity results in a higher level of feeding for the extended family of the subsistence farmer, it is still clearly a good thing – but it does not remove the marketing difficulty from the path of structural change. Where improvements in agricultural productivity occur

* From Hans W. Singer, "Balanced Growth in Economic Development," *Economic Growth: Rationale, Problems, Cases,* ed. Eastin Nelson (Austin, 1960), pp. 81–5. Reprinted by permission of the University of Texas Press.

in relation to commercial crops, and even more so where they occur in relation to export crops, we can be reasonably certain that such improvements will create pre-conditions for growth, and enable us to dispense with the balanced-investment package as a specific remedy for marketing troubles. Where agriculture productivity rises within a system of subsistence farming, it should normally be possible for an enlightened government to link this rise in productivity with institutional changes that would utilize it as a foundation of growth. For example, where the higher agricultural productivity is accompanied by the offer of "incentive goods" to farmers which will induce them to develop a propensity to "truck, barter, and exchange" as their output increases, growth becomes possible as a result. Furthermore, an increase in agricultural productivity, in so far as it releases labor from the farms, creates part of that elasticity of factor supply which makes the balanced-investment package possible.

2) A second road to economic growth is improvement of productivity outside agriculture, specifically in industry. There is plenty of evidence to show enormous scope for such improvement. It would indeed be surprising if it were otherwise, considering the lack of experience in handling capital, the scarcity of managerial skills, the absence of supporting managerial services and of external economies, and the absence of maintenance and repair facilities. We may perhaps add to this list the fact that the technology used is an alien growth imported from abroad, and was therefore not developed in line with the requirements and resource endowments of the underdeveloped countries. . . . Such nonagricultural improvements may be not so obvious, especially to the outside observer, as the need for higher productivity in agriculture. But even though agriculture may employ 70 per cent to 80 per cent of the total population, it does not normally account for more than half the national income. It follows that a given degree of improvement in the nonagricultural sectors will increase total real incomes by about as much as the same degree of agricultural improvement. Investments designed to raise nonagricultural productivity, by lowering real cost curves, will create "markets" where none existed before, and they do so without the need for a broadly based investment package.

3) The promotion of export trade is a third means of stimulating economic growth. The low-level equilibrium deadlock of real incomes and markets exists only in a closed economy, or for the world as a whole. In any individual underdeveloped country with significant foreign trade — and that means nearly all underdeveloped countries — some of the markets lie abroad in highly developed countries, and

hence are not limited by the low domestic incomes. These markets are, of course, also limited: by real incomes abroad, by competition from possibly lower cost competitors, and by technological changes. Furthermore, the notorious instability of world commodity prices may make markets abroad particularly hazardous for the specialized exporter. All the same, export promotion offers a historically and analytically most important method of by-passing the marketing deadlock, offering opportunities for economic growth without the balanced-investment package.

4) A fourth means of improving the economic status of an underdeveloped country is import substitution. A country engaged in foreign trade has established domestic markets presently supplied by imports from abroad. Import substitution, like export promotion, thus offers an opportunity of growth in happy disregard of the need for an investment package. The protective tariff has historically been a major alternative to the balanced-investment package, in the early stages of development. Arthur Lewis' "Report on the Industrialization of the Gold Coast" provides the *locus classicus* for this unbalanced, yet effective, approach.

5) In relation to the improvement of productivity, there is a fifth approach to economic growth, via building up the economic infrastructure. Here, perhaps, investment in transport facilities is most obviously an alternative to the balanced-investment package as a method of creating new markets. The absence of markets in underdeveloped countries is not merely a question of the specific economic framework and institutions in which the incomes are earned. If the division of labor depends on the extent of the market, the market in turn depends on the extent to which certain facilities are available. Transport is the most obvious of these facilities. The doctrine of balanced economic growth is right in emphasizing the creation of markets as a key problem, but one can create markets by methods other than by inducing balanced demand.

6) Unbalanced investment, a sixth means of encouraging economic growth, and quite apart from foreign trade, appears at first paradoxical. It would be unrealistic to assume a state of perfect harmony—even the harmony of the deadlock—between markets and supplies. The doctrine of balanced growth seems to assume that in making decisions on the allocation of resources in an underdeveloped country we start from scratch. That, of course, is not so. Rather, we start with a situation which incorporates the effects of previous investment and previous developments. This means that at any given point of time there are types of investment which are not in them-

selves balanced-investment packages, but which are complementary to existing investments, and which thus bring the total stock of capital nearer balance. We must thus distinguish between balance as the end result at which to aim, and balance as the method of approach. Where you start with imbalance, you need further imbalance in order to come closer to balance. It may be said that this still leaves the concept of the balanced-investment package valid, only stretching it over several investment periods. Thus, while we may be aiming at balance as an investment criterion, we achieve this objective by unbalanced investment.

We have now described six alternative approaches other than those singled out by the doctrine of "balanced growth." Each of these alternative approaches could conceivably, if successfully pursued, resolve the marketing deadlock which gave origin to the doctrine of balanced growth. Thus balanced growth should be judged not as a sole cure for the evil correctly diagnosed but as one of several possible cures. Which of the various cures will be the most appropriate will then depend on specific situations, and more particularly on the total volume of available resources. In this respect, the specific cure of the balanced-investment package does not compare well in the early stages of development because it requires large resources—in fact larger resources than most expositors of the doctrine seem to realize. The balanced-investment package cannot logically be confined to a group of projects which are self-supporting on the demand side; the package must include investment in agriculture and in the infrastructure. The cure is far from being the sole cure; in addition, it is an expensive cure and one which is most effective when taken as a mixture with other prescriptions.

But having thus defined the limitations of the doctrine, we are now perhaps in a better position also to appreciate its merits: the combination of self-supporting projects can serve to raise the productivity of investment. In particular, it can prevent the creation of "white elephants"—projects without a market—which dot the landscape in so many underdeveloped countries. As between alternative appropriations of *given* resources, the balanced-investment package has an inherent superiority—wherever the available resources are sufficient for such a package.

There is another lesson which we can learn from the doctrine of balanced growth. The inducement to invest will be greatly increased by expectation of expanding markets and expanding incomes. Inflationary expectations are one way of increasing the inducement to invest; an expectation of real growth would be just as effective – perhaps more effective. It is not sufficient that complementary investment which will provide markets actually go forward; it is necessary also that it be seen or known, or at least assumed, to go forward. For this reason, in any development program of an underdeveloped country it is crucially important to create a general sense of moving forward. The very formulation of development programs may be helpful in creating such a sense of moving forward – more specifically, I believe that this is also one of the most important effects of the community development movement in India. Balanced growth can play a part in improving what in trade cycle theory is perhaps rather vaguely called "the state of business confidence." A low-level deadlock of incomes and markets can be due to excessive self-justifying pessimism concerning future markets, particularly where there is a long history of stagnation or economic troubles. It is, however, not so easy for excessive optimism to be self-justifying – the inexorable limitation of resources stands in the way. Where the low-level equilibrium has been determined by excessive pessimism rather than by resource limitation, the doctrine of balanced growth acquires considerable theoretical as well as practical merit.

Finally, let us remember that the objections to the doctrine of balanced growth will be greatly reduced and finally vanish as the available resources increase in the course of economic growth. Thus interpreted, the doctrine should stimulate underdeveloped countries to undertake the necessary sacrifices in the early stages of development; it dangles before them a carrot – the hope that one day when resources have become big enough, balanced-investment packages will become possible. Having labored to the top, the balanced-investment package will help them to "slide down the other side of the roof," into the promised land of cumulative growth and compound interest.

PART FOUR

THE ALLOCATION OF CAPITAL

INTRODUCTION

The problem of allocation is to ensure that the developing nation gets the maximum benefit from that volume of capital which it has been able to accumulate. In a purely market economy, the allocation of investment is governed by entrepreneurs interpreting market prices to discover the specific projects which will yield the greatest return to the scare resource—capital. Unfortunately, there is no guarantee that capital will not be wasted by this allocation process: current prices are frequently very imperfect guides to future prices and the rate of return to capital will depend upon the prices prevailing when the investment has actually become productive. Further, future prices are available in only a very few markets so that there does not exist an all-embracing system of prices to serve as a guide to investment allocation. Sometimes the price system fails to take into account the interdependence of sectors and the repercussions on the costs and benefits of these interdependencies. In a developed economy (which is better able to afford a suboptimal allocation of capital) these interdependencies are unlikely to be as important as in a poor economy; thus the price system may be considered as generally less reliable in poor countries.

The allocation criterion most commonly suggested is the maximizing of the *social* marginal product of each available lump of capital. However, the actual criterion by which an all-knowing planner would allocate the disposable capital, would vary in accordance with the planner's goals and with his time horizon. The importance of using a criterion based on social product rather than private product becomes more marked when the case for investment in social overhead capital and in education and other forms of human capital are considered. Investment in these areas is extremely difficult to incorporate into a criterion based on private profit.

The future requirement of poor nations for foreign goods and services must be met from future earnings of foreign exchange from exports, reserves, foreign gifts or loans, or capital imports. Since loans and capital imports necessarily imply interest and dividend payments which impair the earnings from exports, it is argued that any investment criterion must take into account the necessity of either expanding the proceeds from exports or reducing the need for imports. To the extent that the rate of exchange is arbitrarily fixed, the price mechanism cannot be relied upon to measure the relative desirability of foreign and domestic goods. In fact, the balance of payments constraint on the investment criterion is usually taken care of by a combination of an overvalued currency, encouraging exports, and high tariffs on imports, encouraging domestic production of import substitutes; the overvaluation of the currency necessitating control over expenditures on foreign goods by some agency of the government. This, some economists argue, leads to more and more government regulation and controls in economies where able administrators are few and already overburdened with the tasks of providing absolutely essential governmental services. The inefficiencies of inadequate government bureaucracies may be as bad or worse than the inefficiencies of markets.

It is easier for economists to agree on the shortcomings of the private marginal product as a proper criterion for investment for society than on an alternative criterion. Harvey Leibenstein discusses why the current state of economic knowledge does not warrant calling some criterion *the* proper one for an underdeveloped country to follow. Substitution of social marginal productivity and cost for private marginal productivity and cost does not settle the issue. It merely suggests, Leibenstein points out, "that there may be some valuations which for society as a whole are different from the valuations as determined by private decision-making entities. . . . It does not tell us, nor does it spell out, what are the factors to be taken into account in the determination of social valuations rather than the private valuations. Clearly on this latter aspect, there may be legitimate differences of opinion."

The United Nations analyzes the problem facing any developing society concerning the proper allocations of its scarce investible resources between directly productive activities such as factories and agriculture and the " 'physical infrastructure' or 'overhead capital for the economy as a whole' such as transport and power, etc.," which are necessary for the successful conduct of directly productive activities. The answer is different for each country depending upon the stage of its development, the relative strength of the private and public sectors, and the structural needs of its economy. The article also examines an aspect of the balanced-unbalanced growth controversy: whether balanced investments in these two sectors are better than unbalanced investments for generating rapid growth.

Myint points out that most underdeveloped countries are concentrating their efforts on raising investment rates and establishing substantial manufacturing to meet Rostow's two conditions of take-off but are ignoring the task of fulfilling a third and critical Rostovian condition, i.e., of creating "a political, social and institutional framework which exploits the impulses to expansion in the modern sector and the potential external economy effects of the take-off and gives to growth an ongoing character." Few of these countries, economists, or social scientists, including Rostow, have done much to explore "the no-man's land between anthropology and economics" which must be cultivated if the preconditions for take-off are to be created.

Two conflicting requirements for economic development Myint argues, are social flexibility and social discipline which call for investment allocations. Wrong investments in material capital can be scrapped. "Wrong pieces of human capital cannot be scrapped; they tend to be self-perpetuating and have the habit of not merely distorting but actually disrupting the social infrastructure." Hence the great need to evolve proper guidelines for allocating capital between physical and the social infrastructures of a society and between the different elements of the social infrastructure.[1]

[1] Irving Swerdlow, in *Development Administration — Concepts and Problems* (Syracuse, 1963), pp. 106–111, at once widens and narrows the focus. While Myint's concern is with the development of social and political ingredients for promoting economic development, Swerdlow points to the necessity of looking at economic development as an aspect of the larger process of social modernization. He then narrows the focus on the critical need to invest in the development

Theodore W. Schultz narrows the focus by arguing that underdeveloped countries are spending far too little on the building up of their human capital through education and training of their peoples and spending disproportionately on physical capital. Citing studies of underdeveloped and developed countries, he makes the case that "technical advances are the key factor in advancing rapid development and that additional expenditures to improve the quality of the [technically trained] labor force are of primary importance in attaining this end."

HARVEY LEIBENSTEIN

Why Do We Disagree on Investment Policies for Development?*

I. INTRODUCTION

The question of investment policy for the economic development of underdeveloped areas is still, at least in my opinion, a very much unsettled matter. That this should be the case is hardly surprising since the "correct policy," if such exists, depends on the solution of a number of intellectual problems that have as yet not been solved. It is *not* my purpose, in this paper, to set forth and argue for the "correct" investment allocation policy. On the contrary I hope to show that given the present imperfect state of our knowledge with respect to the factors that are significant in economic development

of adequate and effective public administrations and the adoption of economic policies which solve problems with minimum demands on scarce administrative capacity.

* From Harvey Leibenstein, "Why Do We Disagree on Investment Policies for Development?," *Indian Economic Journal* (April 1958), pp. 369–386. Reprinted by permission of the author and of the *Indian Economic Journal.*

it is impossible to come to a definitive conclusion on this matter. Different scholars may be warranted in holding different positions with respect to investment policies. If this be so then it follows that the "orthodox position," i.e., the position that emphasizes the *usual* interpretation of the marginal productivity criterion, has not been demonstrated to be the correct one, nor, by the same token, has any alternative position been proven to be correct beyond any shadow of doubt. Perhaps this is platitudinous and obvious. I hope so. But some of the recent, and not so recent literature on the subject, as well as both casual and serious conversations with a number of economists, has suggested to me that this is not quite the case. Many appear to hold very strong views on the matter – often very much stronger than our present knowledge would seem to warrant. It is this feeling that prompts the present attempt to analyze why different investigators may logically and reasonably reach different conclusions on this question.

II. ALTERNATIVE DECISION ENVIRONMENTS

Apart from errors in logic there are two main reasons why people come to, or appear to come to, different conclusions with respect to the same problem; different interpretations of significant concepts, or because they start from different premises. We shall leave until later the matter of semantics. The matter of premises or assumptions is far from simple in this connection. What is involved, often implicitly, is not a difference in a single assumption, or a single set of assumptions of the *same* kind, but different premises and views of the problem that come under a variety of headings. Indeed, the word assumptions or premises may be misleading in this connection, and therefore I shall use the notion of a "decision environment" to indicate what I have in mind. The following schematic outline indicates what I mean by a decision environment, and the discussion that follows suggests its relevance to the investment decision problem.

SCHEMATIC OUTLINE OF THE PROBLEM

A. The Situation or Situation Class

B. The Decision Environment

Normative Aspects

1. Social objective or objectives

(a) General statement of the objective(s)

(b) Side conditions or constraints on the objective or its components

(c) Means of evaluating components of the objective(s)

2. Values, restraints, and views, regarding the use of instruments to achieve the objective(s)
3. Time commitment and conditions connected with the time elements

Economic Aspects

1. Target variables through which one judges the objective and its furtherance
2. View of the economic system
(a) Equation system
(b) Characteristics of the behavior equations
(c) Assessment of the value of the parameters
3. Costs, benefits, and effects of direct (and permissible) instruments

C. *Policy*

The outline suggests the main elements that may be involved in an investment policy. The specific economic situation that the country finds itself in is, of course, a crucial factor. That is to say, it would be foolish to make a specific investment allocation without taking into account the specific facts at the time the decision is made. On a higher level of abstraction we would consider a class of situations that a country might find itself in, and attempt to establish investment criteria for that class. But the point of this paper is that a knowledge of the situation is not enough to determine an investment decision, nor is a knowledge of the characteristics of the situation class sufficient to determine investment criteria. Other matters are vitally involved, and it is these other matters that I refer to as the decision environment. In a short paper one cannot be exhaustive. The points listed in the outline above are intended only to be suggestive. However, they are probably sufficient to show why reasonable and logical men who agree on the situation class might very well disagree on investment policies. But we should not jump to any conclusions at this stage. There is more to the problem than simply the fact that different individuals may differ with respect to the decision environment.

The decision environment can be divided into two parts: A normative aspect, and an economic one. The division is far from perfect, and we may argue about its exact boundary, but it will do for our purposes. One aspect of the decision environment depends on norms, aims, values, and so on. It depends on the social goals and value of the society. To that extent it is normative rather than objective or scientific. On the other hand, the economic aspect depends on our view of how the economy operates. If economies were a completed science, and all the necessary facts were available, then we might all agree on the economic aspect, although we might still differ on the normative aspect.

1. Consider the problem of choosing the development objective. There are a large number of possible objectives. But the problem is also complicated by the fact that the statement of such objectives will have a number of dimensions. For example we may consider maximizing the aggregate output stream, or the aggregate *per capita* income stream or the aggregate *per capita* consumption stream, or the average length of life, etc. But statements such as these are usually incomplete. One problem is the treatment of time. In other words, if we consider the maximization of the aggregate output stream, the question arises over what period of time it is to be maximized. Usually, we conceive of some discounting procedure and attempt to maximize the present value of the output stream. In any event something has to be said in the statement of the objective as to how the time dimension is to be handled.

Another complicating feature lies in the fact that the variable to be maximized is rarely to be considered by itself in the absence of all other considerations. In other words, what we usually ask to do is to maximize some variable subject to a number of stated constraints. Thus we might attempt to maximize the present value of the output stream subject to the constraint that the income distribution is not worsened in the process.

The objective may have more than one component (or variable) that is to be optimized. In that event some way of assessing the relative importance of different components has to be determined. Clearly, economists, as well as citizens, might differ on the appropriate objectives for development.

2. Development is not an ultimate objective that supersedes all other considerations. Not all possible means to achieve given ends are legitimate. We shall see that the constraints that we impose on the means that we can employ may affect our investment policy.

What is involved here is in part the age old question between agenda and non-agenda. That is to say, with respect to what variables are we to assume that the government or the state can interfere and control and what variables are we to assume are determined by the freely chosen actions and activities of the individuals involved? We shall also see that these sets of questions are in part related to our view of the development processes.

This point may perhaps best be indicated by a few examples. We may assume, for example, that the size of the population is determined entirely from within the system. Or we may assume that the population size can somehow be controlled by governmental action and that therefore it is a variable whose value is determined exogenously. Another possibility is that the level of consumption of population is determined within the system. Or we may assume that it is determined in part socially through a system of taxes and subsidies. Similarly we may perhaps argue that the rate of saving is determined by individual action or that it is determined by government interference. In general we can see that with respect to many variables we can make either an assumption of control or an assumption of lack of control. It will turn out that in some instances, *but not all*, we get different results depending on which set of assumptions we make.

3. The time element enters the problem in a variety of ways. At the extremes we might consider a single, once and for all investment decision apart from any other decision, as against an investment policy to cover an infinite series of investment decisions. We shall see that there are cases where it does make a distinct difference whether the decision or criterion to be applied is with respect to an isolated case, or part of a series of decisions.

4. If the social objective is stated in broad terms then there arises the problem of interpreting the objective in terms of one or more economic variables. For example, if our objective is to maximize the "standard of living" of the populace, how is this to be interpreted in economic terms? For example, how is leisure to be valued in such circumstances? We shall not go into detail in this matter, but clearly there are great possibilities for differences of opinion in this regard.

5. Really significant differences may arise with respect to our view of the development process. What will be the train of consequences that will result from a given investment allocation? The theory of economic growth is not at present in such a state that all would readily agree on this matter. The number of possible dynamical systems that we could invent is certainly very large. Given different views of economic development processes we may (but need not always) arrive at different investment criteria. We will see that whether or not different development theories lead to different criteria will depend, in part, on the other components of the decision environment.

6. The employment of direct instruments, for example, the attempt by the state to determine directly the rate of savings, or the birth rate, is usually not costless, although such costs are often ignored in discussions. Economists may legitimately differ on the costs and

consequences of direct instruments, even in those cases where the normative aspects of the decision environment permits their use. The importance of this aspect will become clearer as we proceed.

There are an infinite number of decision environments that are possible. Obviously, it would be too tedious and time consuming to consider one by one all the possible decision environments that can be obtained by varying slightly its components. As a result we shall limit ourselves to examining only a few possibilities, picked in part because they help to illustrate some interesting points.

We will find that there does not exist a one-to-one correspondence between the alternative combinations of objectives, theories, socially determined parameters, etc., and the allocation criteria that can be deduced from them. Rather, we shall see that there are many-to-one correspondences. Namely, there are sets of combinations which lead to different criteria. That is to say we can outline a set of objectives, theories, and social constraints, and so on, for which a given allocation criteria may be correct for each of the combinations within the set. But there is more than one such set, and as a consequence there is more than one "reasonable" allocation criterion. However, the fact that there are often a number of decision environments consistent with a given criterion may sometimes have given the impression that the criterion is universally (or almost universally) applicable.

III. THE INVESTMENT ALLOCATION PROBLEM

Before we proceed any further it is well to indicate the exact nature of the problem we have in mind. We begin with a given decision environment. Next, we assume that there is a given investment fund available, and that some central agency is in a position to influence or determine the allocation strategy. We differentiate between the allocation strategy and the mechanism of allocation. These are really two separate matters, although they are in some cases related to each other. For present purposes we are concerned only with allocation strategies and not with the question of the optimal mechanism under which to carry out the appropriate strategy. Thus we are not concerned with whether the government actually makes the allocations, or whether these are made through the mechanism of private enterprisers operating on their own, or operating under a system of subsidies and taxes, etc.

The given investment fund available at the outset can be allocated among a number of industries or uses. The two main aspects of the allocation problem solved simultaneously, in practice, are (1) the allocation between industries and (2) the allocation among techniques. Any concrete allocation must involve choosing the technique while one chooses simultaneously the industry. But to simplify the discussion we shall assume, except where we specifically indicate otherwise, that the allocation is to be made among industries. That is, we assume that for each industry the technique of production is given, unless otherwise stated.[1]

Now we have to distinguish between an "allocation plan" and an "allocation." By an allocation plan we have in mind any specific allocation of the investment fund among the industries. Thus if A is an allocation plan, we may write $a_i, \ldots a_k$ as the details of this allocation plan. In other words, a_i denotes the amount of the investment fund that is to be used for the addition of capital in the ith industry. We view a_i as a specific allocation and A as an allocation plan. There are, of course, innumerable allocation plans that are possible and our problem is to pick that allocation plan which most meets the objective contained in the decision environment. The general allocation problem is to find a criterion or principle (i.e., a strategy) by which to order or rank alternative allocation plans. Usually the allocation plans are in themselves of so complex a nature, or their consequences taken as a whole are so complex, that it is not possible to rank alternative plans directly. An alternative (and usual) procedure is to find a means of evaluating the consequences, for example, the income stream, of a specific allocation. By comparing the consequences of alternative allocations, and by shifting units of investment from one allocation to another until the consequences are equated at the margin an optimum is obtained. In this manner the ranking of allocation plans is achieved indirectly.

More specifically, the usual scheme is to assume that there is a specific consequence that follows from a specific allocation. Let us write c_i for the consequence that follows from the allocation a_i. Once we know the set of consequences c_i, for all i, and once we are able to tell what happens when we shift a small amount of investment from industry i to industry j, or *vice versa,* we are then able to apply the well known equi-marginal principles in order to obtain a maximum.[2] But it is important to observe that this really does not tell

[1] We can get around this problem by defining "industry" in such a way so that the production of a commodity with a different technique implies a different industry. The reader may substitute this interpretation for the one in the text if he wishes.

[2] At no point should we argue against the applicability of the equimarginal

us very much about the solution of the problem in any concrete situation. What it does do is merely suggest some of the questions that have to be answered in order to approach a solution. For example, (1) What are the consequences to be considered for any specific allocation? (2) How are these consequences generated by the economic system as a whole? That is to say, how do we visualize the process that generates the stream of consequences resulting from a specific allocation? (3) Are the consequences unique and unalterable by social action or can they be changed, to some extent, by interference of a social agency? (4) For any given allocation what is the variety and range of consequences and how are these consequences related to each other? etc.

The time element enters the problem in several significant ways. We have already alluded to the fact that the time factor may enter implicitly or explicitly in the determination of the development objective. One consequence of this is that we have to devise means by which to judge alternate output streams; for example, through a discounting technique, that enables us to evaluate alternate streams in terms of their present values.

But the time element enters the picture in a more fundamental sense. There is a time aspect to our view of the allocation problem. Namely, are we to be concerned with a single allocation plan or a sequence of them? That is, the determination of the allocation plan for one year may be very different, if we determine it as a once-and-for-all matter, apart from future plan, or if we determine it in connection with a series of future plans. In other words, the strategy for a single year need not be the same as the strategy for that year when we are simultaneously considering the strategy for *n* years.

Now, the time elements probably determine the extent to which the indirect effects of an allocation plan should be taken into account. It is likely that the greater the time period that is considered the more significant are the indirect aspects of the problem, and the less applicable are the *ceteris paribus* assumptions. But the longer the series of allocation decisions to be made, the greater the possibility of taking into account and influencing some of the indirect effects.

principle, or some variant thereof. The appropriateness of the calculus to maximum problems is not in question. Even in those cases where it appears that the marginal productivity criterion is not applicable, we should not argue against the "marginal" aspect of the criterion. The argument rather is always to be understood to be with respect to the content of the criterion and not the application of the marginal concept as such. The marginal concept may be said to be contentless. Economists' arguments should not be about the mathematics of maximization.

We now state in a few words the crux of our analysis. We distinguish between the *direct* and *indirect* consequences that we attribute to specific allocations. By a direct consequence we have in mind the increase in the output stream in a given industry that results from the allocation of investment to that industry. The indirect consequences are all of the other effects that may be attributed to this allocation, either by itself or in connection with the rest of a specified allocation plan, or series of plans. The heart of the matter is whether the indirect consequences are significant for development purposes. The differences between the few models that we shall elaborate, and the allocation criteria appropriate to them, and between a host of other possible models, will rest almost entirely on the extent to which the indirect consequences of given allocation are taken into account.

To elaborate this idea, we might specify briefly some of the indirect consequences that come to mind. The allocation plan may affect (1) the future investment as well as the future output stream. (2) It may affect the propensities to consume and the propensities to save. (3) The allocation plan and the accumulation of capital that results thereby, may change the environment in which work takes place and in this way may possibly affect, (a) intensity of effort, (b) the energy of the work force, (c) the degree to which the labour force is willing to adhere to work discipline, (d) the degree to which they develop feather bedding and innovation-retarding practices, (e) the nature of work morale, (f) the degree of economic and social mobility, and a host of other similar factors. (4) The allocation, by affecting the structure of capital, will affect the productivity of the labour force from the point of view of establishing a new relationship between the capital structure and the skill structure of the work force. (5) Finally, the allocation plan, and its consequent capital accumulation, may affect the social and cultural environment under which the economy operates, and in turn affect various aspects of the quality of the population. We shall elaborate on some of these matters as we proceed.

IV. SOME ALTERNATIVE MODELS CONSIDERED

If there were no space and time limitations, then we might consider, one by one, a large number of decision environments. But in view of such limitations a rather brief characterization and comparison of only a few decision environments will have to suffice. We shall consider two for which the social marginal productivity criterion is correct, and then sketch one environment for which the social marginal productivity criterion does not apply. Finally we shall discuss some of the critical elements that would determine the applicability of social marginal productivity or other criteria.

Model 1 — A neo-classical type model. For our first decision environment we shall assume: (1) that the objective of development is to maximize the present value of the *aggregate* output stream; and (2) that there exists some acceptable discounting procedure, and discount rate.

The theory we have in mind for this particular decision environment is that which comes closest to the static, conventional, microeconomic (textbook variety) model of the economic process. We assume the existence of factors of production, human and nonhuman, which form the stock of potential inputs. These inputs are combined in the production process in order to yield the stream of outputs. Investment, in this model, is defined as the net addition to the stock of nonhuman inputs. It is further assumed that during the time period involved the quality, size, and nature of the work force remains constant.

The consequence of investment, in this case, is simply, and only, to add to the stock of capital goods. The allocation problem here is reduced to a comparison of those income streams that result as a consequence of alternate allocation plans, and to the choice of a strategy that leads to that allocation plan whose output stream has a present value that is equal to or greater than that of all alternative allocation plans. The conventional marginal productivity principle is clearly effective here. The allocation of funds to a given industry results in an increase in the present value of that output stream. At the margin one can determine the present value of the output stream that results from the marginal input of investment in that industry. By comparing the marginal productivities thus defined, that is, the addition to the present value of the output stream that results from the application of a marginal increment to the capital stock, and allocating the capital fund so that the marginal productivities are equal for all industries, we maximize the addition to the output stream.

In this case only the *direct* consequences of any specific allocation are taken into account. Note the assumption that the total consequences of an allocation plan are no larger than the sum of direct consequences of each of the specific allocations. That is to say, there are no social economies or social diseconomies that enter the picture. The marginal productivity of an allocation and the *social* marginal productivity of that allocation are one and the same thing in this particular case. However, this is not always the situation, and we must allow for those instances.

It is not altogether clear from the literature how the word "social" in "social marginal productivity" is to be interpreted. There are at least two meanings that we could attach to the adjective "social." (1) We can assume that the marginal product of an allocation has a different social valuation than its individual private valuation. This may be because of effects of the production activity which are not taken into account in determining private costs and prices. The usual examples are such things as smoke nuisances, noise, etc. There exist in production processes costs which, because of their nature, are not borne privately. Likewise there may be social benefits of the same nature.

The other meaning that may be attached to the adjective "social," in this context, is that the output of the allocation plan is not the same as the sum of the outputs of each of the individual allocations, when they are considered apart from the other allocations that make up the allocation plan. This involves the well-known complementarities of production between industries.

Assuming that we add into our evaluation of the marginal product the differences between the social valuation and the private valuation we then obtain the application of the well-known social marginal productivity criterion. It is to be observed that in the first case it is quite simple to add the difference between the social and the private values of the marginal product since these are applied to the specific allocation themselves, apart from the other allocations that occur within the investment plan, while, in the second case, it is much more difficult because we cannot know the social valuation for a given allocation without knowing the rest of the investment plan. That is to say, for every alternative investment plan, there exists an alternative social valuation of the particular allocation under consideration.

The important consideration for our purposes is that it is assumed that the social valuation of a specific allocation depends only on differences between social and private costs, social and private benefits, and on the complementaries of production. Notice that the social valuations of the results of investment do not depend, in this model, on the effects of the allocation plan on the size, nature, quality, or desires of the work force, and populace as such. It is this last aspect that will differentiate, in great part, this decision environment from the one that we shall consider below under model 3.

Model 2 — Neo-classical model — per capita output maximized.

The decision environment we now consider is exactly the same as the one above with the sole exception that the objective of development is to maximize the present value of the *per capita* output stream rather than the present value of the aggregate output stream. It turns out that the result of this case is exactly the same as in the decision environment considered above. This is due to the fact that changes in population and the work force are independent of the allocation plan. Similarly, it follows that any objective involving the population, or some property, characteristic, or a quality of the population, will lead to the same allocation criterion as above as long as such characteristics and properties are assumed to be independent of the allocation plan.

Model 3 – The strong interdependence model. Under this heading we outline a decision environment very different from the ones considered previously.

The objective is the same as in model 2 – namely, the maximization of the present value of the *per capita* output stream. However, the vision of the economic process is very different in this case.

The crucial difference here is that we assume that the allocation plan in the first period will affect a number of variables that were assumed to be independent in the previous models. To be specific we assume that the allocation plan in period one affects in a significant way the following aspects in subsequent periods:

1. The propensity to consume in subsequent periods.
2. The inducement to invest in subsequent periods.
3. The size of the population and labour force in subsequent periods.
4. The quality of the work force in subsequent periods. To be specific, the energy level of the work force, its morale, its responsiveness to discipline, etc. Last but not least, the educational and skill level of the work force.

Once we insert into our decision environment the interdependence of the investment plan in one period and the nature of the inputs in subsequent periods then we have a completely different situation from that in the models considered above. To see this consider for a moment the possibility that arises from the fact that population growth is no longer exogenously determined. For example, allocation plan *A* may maximize the present value of the aggregate output stream but induce a large rate of population growth, while allocation plan *B* may lead to a smaller increase in the aggregate output stream but induce a more than proportionately smaller increase in population growth. Allocation plan *B* will then be preferred to A if our objective is to maximize *per capita* output. The marginal productivity criterion, as this is usually defined, no longer suffices under such circumstances.

At this juncture a semantic note is in order. The concept of productivity is rarely, if ever, considered to be identical with the totality of consequences that follows from a given allocation plan. Rather, by the productivity of a given set of inputs we usually mean the flow of outputs that results directly from the combination of the inputs. It does not take into account other consequences that are not directly related to the flow of outputs. That is to say, it is rarely, if ever, suggested that the concept of productivity should also include the behaviour of the factors of production in their capacities as consumers, investors, procreators, and so on. Clearly this is in accordance with the ordinary and common sense usage of the word "product" and "productivity." Thus it follows that when the aggregate product stream, in the sense just indicated, is not the sole consideration then an allocation criterion that involves only the product stream, (or productivity), such as the marginal productivity criterion, cannot be universally applicable.

The correct allocation criterion under decision environment 3 is much more difficult to determine and state than under the others. Here we have to look for that allocation plan that leads to a time pattern of capital growth *per capita,* and of growth in the quality of the population, again *per capita,* so that the present value of the output stream *per capita* is maximized. There are two streams that are of primary importance. First, we have to consider the regular re-investment stream. That is to say, we have to take into account the extent to which the allocation plan affects the investment rates and amounts, on a *per capita* basis, in the future. Second, we have to consider what might be called the human re-investment stream. That is to say, we have to take into account the extent to which the consumption patterns, as well as the investment patterns, that are consequences of the allocation plan, affect the quality of the population, and in turn, the productive capacity of the population – all of these in *per capita* terms. For present purposes we need not attempt to spell out the exact criterion applicable to this decision environment. It should be clear from the foregoing that many more considerations are involved here than are usually taken into account in the application of the marginal productivity criterion. Certainly the marginal productivity criterion, as defined here, will not always give the correct result under these circumstances.

However, the semantic aspect of the debate must not be lost

sight of. That is to say, part of the argument may have to do with differences in the way we use words. For example, a great deal depends on how we interpret the word "social" in the social marginal productivity criterion. If by social rather than private marginal productivity valuations we are to understand the inclusion of all the factors that we have considered in the last decision environment then, of course, the social marginal productivity criterion will always give the right result. But in this case are we not stretching the meaning and interpretation of the word "social"? It seems to me that the only thing that "social" suggests is the fact that there may be some valuations which for society as a whole are different from the valuations as determined by private decision making entities. All that the adjective "social" really tells us is to be on guard and not accept the private valuations of productivity. It does not tell us, nor does it spell out, what are the factors to be taken into account in the determination of social valuations rather than the private valuations. Clearly, on this latter aspect, there may be legitimate differences of opinion. Problems arise because such differences are often not made explicit.

V. REVIEW OF CRITICAL ELEMENTS

Semantic illusions may lead us to believe that we differ on allocation criteria when in fact we are merely using words differently. But apart from such semantic tangles the difference may be real ones when they are based on different decision environments. However, we have seen that different decision environments are in themselves not always sufficient to lead to different investment criteria. In other words, there is not a one-to-one correspondence between decision environments and appropriate allocation criteria. Rather, there are many decision environments for which the same allocation criterion may be applicable. (It is this feature that may be responsible, in part, for the belief in the near universality of some criteria.) For example, decision model 1 and 2 considered above implied the same allocation criterion and policy although the objectives in these decision environments were different. The reason for this was that the difference in the objectives was connected with a variable (population) that was assumed to be exogenous to the system and hence could not be affected by the investment plan.

Whether or not different decision environments lead to different allocation criteria and policies will depend, in great part, on the interaction between four broad factors: (1) the significance of the indirect consequences of the allocation plan (or plans), (2) the possibilities and costs of using direct social instruments (e.g., government action) to determine the values of variables or parameters, (3) the differences in the view of the economic development process (i.e., in different development theories), and (4) differences in objectives.

(a) *Indirect consequences of allocations and direct social instruments.* Items (1) and (2) above are very closely connected because the operation of the second may nullify the significance of the first. That is, if the indirect consequence of an allocation plan is important, but if the values of the variables or parameters so affected can be altered by the use of direct social instruments which are costless, then the indirect consequences can always be counteracted. For example, compare models 2 and 3 in the previous section. The objectives in both models are the same, but in model 3 some of the indirect consequences of the allocation plan are assumed to be important, and to affect variables (population size, investment rate, etc.) that are assumed to be exogenous to the system in model 2. The two models do imply different investment criteria and policies. But if we had assumed (as part of the decision environment) with respect to model 3 that the government could by direct action determine the size of the population, the quality of the labour force, the rate of investment, and so on, and if the costs of doing so were trivial, then the same investment criteria and policies would have been applicable in both cases. But, of course, some may believe that the use of direct social instruments for some of these purposes may not be possible, or that they should not be used for ideological reasons, or if possible and permissible they may be costlier than taking into account the indirect consequences of the allocation plan. In any event we see that different views about the possibility and efficacy of various types of potential government activities, and their costs, may logically lead to different views about appropriate allocation policies.

(b) *The time aspects of the decision environment.* Whether or not the indirect consequences of an allocation plan (or series of plans) are significant may depend on the time horizon and time commitment aspects of the decision environment. Once again compare models 2 and 3. If the time horizon is very short, say only five years rather than several generations, then the indirect consequences considered in model 3 may be trivial, and the appropriate investment policies may be the same for the two models. That is, it may take some time for the indirect consequences to take hold, so to speak.

Even more important is likely to be the question of the time commitment of the investment policy. For example, consider the possible difference between a one-shot-only investment policy versus one for a whole series of potential investment plans for, say, twenty years. The indirect consequences of a single plan may turn out to be trivial and may perhaps best be ignored. In this case the policies for models 2 and 3 can be the same. But the indirect consequences of a series of investment plans over a twenty year period may be considerable. In this latter case the investment criteria and policies applicable for the two models may be very different indeed. Also, the appropriate investment plan for a given year that is looked upon as a one-shot-only affair, without reference to future investment plans, may be very different from the appropriate investment plan that is part of an integrated series.

The importance of the indirect consequences of an allocation plan is determined, in part, by our views of the development process, which, in turn, is distinguished by the nature and importance of the variables that we assume to be endogenous to such a process. We now consider briefly the treatment of some of these matters.

(c) *Population*. The question of how to treat the population aspect in our decision environment enters in at least two different important respects. If the objective is to maximize some *per capita* variable then the growth of population enters in a significant sense since it determines the denominator of the ratio that determines the *per capita* value. The second sense in which population may enter the problem is that the qualities of the population (in the sense of acquired qualities such as learned skills, education, health, and so on) may change over time and affect some of the target variables. For example, the energy and skills of the population may change over time as a consequence of the pattern of investment, and as a result change the productive capacity of the population.

With respect to population size the usual argument revolves around the fact that fertility patterns of various groups in a population may depend on the roles, especially social, familial, and economic roles, that the individuals composing these groups generally play. For example, urban populations often have different fertility rates than rural populations, white collar groups often have different fertility rates than either rural agricultural groups, or urban manual labourers, and so on. Since the pattern of investment allocation is likely to involve both the demand and supply of the labour, and in turn influence the economic and social role patterns, and the distribution of role patterns, it may in this way also influence the consequent fertility rates of the population. It is through such indirect means that the allocation plan may have an effect on population size and population growth.

More directly the allocation plan may determine both the aggregate output and the level of consumption which in turn may, to a certain extent, influence mortality rates, and therefore the rates of population growth. The main point to be considered here is that there is little question but that we can visualize circumstances in which a connection exists between the allocation plan (or series of plans) and the rate of population growth.

(d) *Investment and reinvestment rates.* In considering the effects of an allocation plan (or plans) we must take into account not only the addition to the output stream that results from the allocation plan (or plans) but also their possible influence on the rates of savings and investment in the future periods. As before the importance of this element depends on whether we look upon the rate of savings and investment as determined exogenously or whether it is determined in part by the social and economic environment created by the sequence of allocation plans. If it is the latter, then we arrive at a different conclusion about investment policy, one that is closer to that considered under model 3 than if it is the former. On *a priori* grounds it would appear that rates of savings and investment depend on income distribution and perhaps on the role composition of the population, and on the social and cultural environment in which the population finds itself. To think of it in terms of extremes the pattern of savings of peasants is likely to be very different from that of socially mobile white collar workers. Also, we might expect that the environment and the role composition of the population may be determined by the allocation plans that take place. As before a lot depends on whether or not we believe the savings and investment rates can be determined by direct governmental action, or the use of other social instruments, and also whether such determination is or is not costless.

(e) *The possible relation of social objectives to the development theory.* A point well worth commenting upon, but one which is quite different from our previous considerations, is the possibility that the objective of development may depend on both the development theory we have in mind and the possibilities of development given the investment fund available. For example, if we believe in the *critical minimum effort thesis* that the author has developed elsewhere[3] then we might take the view that if an investment fund is too small then there may not be any allocation that will lead to sustained development. In this case the objective may be made to depend on whether or not sustained development is possible. If the investment fund is such that a sustained development is a possibility

[3] H. Leibenstein, *Economic Backwardness and Economic Growth,* John Wiley and Sons, New York, Chapter 8.

then we might allocate the investment fund in accordance with policies that lead to high rate of reinvestment in the near future, and as a consequence not raise the consumption of the population in the early periods to the level that it might have achieved without the higher investment rate. On the other hand, if the investment fund is too small to generate sustained development, then we may decide that since development is not of the question in any event, that we should concentrate our efforts on maximizing the consumption level of the population even if in the long run this leads eventually to a return to the previous rate of consumption. We shall not elaborate on this aspect of the problem but merely point to the fact that appropriate investment policies may depend, under some circumstances, on criteria other than the maximization of the output stream.

(f) *Population and labour force qualities.* A second variable (or set of variables) of significance that is usually not considered in static or short run economic analysis is the changes in the quality of the population, in the resulting labour force, and in all of the characteristics and properties that we may associate with the notion of acquired population qualities. We cannot take up every aspect that might come under this global concept, but an enumeration of a few might indicate what we have in mind. Some of the qualities that may be of significance for productive purposes are the energy of the population, the acquired skills of the population, the flexibility of the labour force, the economic and social mobility of the population, and the general responsiveness of the population to economic incentives, and so on. The question that arises is whether changes in these properties are independent of the allocation plans that occur, and hence of the investment policies that determine them. It must be clear that we can think of some possibilities under which the allocation plans would affect the qualities of the population. For example, the nature and variety of consumption goods, which are, in part, determined by the allocation plans, will in turn have their influence on the energy level of the population. Also, expenditures on such things as education and educational facilities will in part determine the acquired skills of the population, and their productive capacities. Similarly, the environment created by a series of allocation plans, may, in part, determine the psychological attitudes of the population as well as their flexibility, mobility, and responsiveness to economic incentives.

A central aspect of the view just presented is that the qualities considered are entirely acquired rather than innate. They are characteristics that are determined by the social and economic environment under which the population lives, and in part, determined by the expenditure patterns of the population as such. But the expenditure patterns, both of an investment and consumption kind, may be determined in part by the nature of the allocation plans that take place. Thus we see that an obvious relationship between these elements and investment policy exists. Whether this relationship is really significant or not may be a debatable matter. But clearly our view of what investment policy is appropriate will depend on whether the elements that we have just considered are looked upon as endogenous or exogenous variables within our theory.

In this general connection we may look at model 3 as one that is consistent with the view that economic development involves not only growth in the capital stock, looked at in terms of the aggregate valuation of the physical non-human assets of the economy, but also that it depends on the transformation of the labour force and population as such. That is to say, the nature of industrial populations, the stimuli to which they respond, their energy, the motivations that lie behind their behaviour, as well as the things that they value and the skills that they possess, are very different from that of the typical peasant population that forms so large a part of the population in the typical underdeveloped area. If this type of transformation is looked upon as the paramount phenomenon of development then it would seem to follow that model 3 is more appropriate than the others considered.

On the other hand, if we view the process of development as something that does not affect in any marked degree the population as such, then of course model 1 and 2 may be adequate. It is to be noted, of course, that we may accept the view about the importance of the transformation of the population as part of the process of development and yet not accept the appropriateness of model 3. This would be correct if we believed that such a transformation occurs independently of the allocation plans in the initial and subsequent periods. In other words even if we accept the view that the transformation of the acquired qualities of the population is of paramount importance, we may believe that such a transformation is entirely socially (or governmentally) determinable. That is to say, it can be achieved directly without in any way involving the investment plans within any period, or it may be achieved through exogenous factors or influences that are primarily functions of time but which in no way are related to the investment plans period by period. Which view is correct is the subject for another occasion. Here we merely suggest that these are some of the issues that may be at the heart of the debate over appropriate investment allocation policies.

Physical Infrastructure *vs.* Directly Productive Activities*

AMONG investments in the field of economic development, a major division exists between investment in "physical infrastructure" or "overhead capital for the economy as a whole," such as transport, power, etc., and investment in directly productive activities, such as agriculture, manufacturing industry, etc. The proportion of investment as between these two broad fields in the public investment programme of any given country, should be appraised in the light of the corresponding proportion in the private sector. In a country where the private sector is relatively large, government investment in "directly productive activities" is bound to be proportionally less than in a country where the private sector is relatively small. Government investment in physical infrastructure, especially transport and power, is, however, not so flexible. In developing countries, such investment is not attractive to private entrepreneurs, because returns are small and the amount of capital required is generally beyond their capacity. Yet basic economic facilities are needed in almost every type of production, and their benefits to other sectors of the economy are immense. As the marginal social benefits are so much in excess of marginal private benefits, government investment in these fields has, therefore, invariably ranked high in all development plans of countries of the region.

The high share of investment in transport and communications among all economic sectors is a common feature of almost all current plans. Even in the group of countries (Ceylon, India, Pakistan and the Philippines) with the lowest proportions, it accounted for about one-fourth of the total public investment. In these countries, existing transport facilities meeting present needs appear to be relatively more adequate than in other countries where the existing transport means are either insufficient to meet present needs or future demand as a

* From United Nations, Economic Commission for Asia and the Far East, "A Decade of Development Planning and Implementation," *Economic Bulletin for Asia and the Far East* (December 1961), pp. 8–10.

result of economic expansion, or require substantial rehabilitation. In six countries of the region (Burma, Cambodia, Iran, Nepal, Thailand and south Viet-Nam), the share of investment in transport and communications is 40–50 per cent. To some extent, the relatively high figures reflect the much larger share of public than private investment in this particular branch of physical infrastructure.

The share of power development in total physical investment outlays of the government sector is relatively low in current plans. The Federation of Malaya ranks the highest, with 27 per cent, followed by Pakistan, the Philippines, south Viet-Nam and India with 16–20 per cent, and Burma, Cambodia, Ceylon and Nepal, with 10–15 per cent.

The external economies argument behind the strategy of heavy investment in basic economic facilities presupposes that development in directly productive activities, especially in manufacturing industry, has been hampered by the lack of transport facilities or power supply. While this appears to be true in some countries or some areas in a particular country, with private enterprise, an adequate market organization and sufficient final demand, the strategy may not work in areas where these elements of ability to invest are lacking. Under the latter conditions, excess investment in physical infrastructure may result in extensive idle capacity for at least some time before "the ability to invest" grows sufficiently. It may happen, for instance, that a highway is built before it is justified by the volume of traffic, so that it is little used and therefore left without adequate maintenance. Such idle capacity is clearly a waste of resources which could be devoted more productively to agriculture or industry.

Thus in the Eight-Year Development Plan of Burma, heavy investment in electric power and transport and communications, amounting to 77 per cent of the total public investment in economic sectors, appeared to be excessive. It is reflected in the comparatively low rate of growth with a high rate of investment (high capital/output ratio), and the intensification of the foreign exchange scarcity.

It is therefore not without reason that questions of the following kind were raised: "if we endow an under-developed country with a first-class highway network, with extensive hydroelectric and perhaps irrigation facilities, can we be certain that industrial and agricultural activity will expand in the wake of these improvements? Would it not be less risky and more economical first to make sure of such activity, even though it may have to be subsidized in view of the absence of adequate transportation and power, and then let the ensuing pressures determine the appropriate outlays for SOC (social overhead capital) and its location?"[1]

However, this "pressures" approach also has its disadvantages. Physical infrastructure projects, such as roads, railways and hydroelectric power stations are generally large projects characterized by bulkiness. Their construction requires a rather long time. If it has to wait until demand for their services has accumulated to the extent of exercising pressure, time may be lost and the time required to extend other needed assistance to directly productive fields prolonged. Such assistance, regardless of its form (subsidies, protection, etc.) also amounts to a waste. Moreover, the response to public pressure of the authorities responsible for providing physical infrastructure tends to be weak and slow in under-developed countries. There are many examples of power plants, even of moderate capacity, which took a rather long time to complete, although the authorities concerned seemed not to mind much about the complaints of the public.

Balanced development between physical infrastructure and directly productive fields appears to be an inevitable conclusion. The actual implementation of this general principle depends, to a large extent, on a continuous and accurate assessment of the growth in both sectors, and on timely adjustments in the planning and implementation of the individual projects concerned. In this connexion, it is important that a projection of the future demand for transport services, power and other basic economic facilities should first be made on the basis of the projected or planned growth of the directly productive activities.

[1] A. O. Hirschman, *The Strategy of Economic Development* (Yale University Press, 1959), p. 93.

HLA MYINT

Investment in the Social Infrastructure*

MOST underdeveloped countries aspire to "take off" in the manner described by Professor Rostow, but only a few are ready for the process in the sense that they are anywhere near fulfilling all three of the related conditions he has laid down for a successful take-off. These are: "(a) a rise in the rate of productive investment from (say) 5 per cent or less to over 10 per cent of national income (or net national product); (b) the development of one or more substantial manufacturing sectors, with a high rate of growth; (c) the existence or quick emergence of a political, social and institutional framework which exploits the impulses to expansion in the modern sector and the potential external economy effects of the take-off and gives to growth an ongoing character."[1]

The underdeveloped countries trying to accelerate their economic growth generally turn their attention to Professor Rostow's conditions (a) and (b). They tend to ignore the elusive condition (c) which turns out to be the most important of the three in the sense that unless it is fulfilled to some degree it is not possible to keep the two other conditions fulfilled for long. Thus, according to the historical instances given by Professor Rostow of the countries which have successfully taken off in the past, condition (a) means not merely raising the rate of capital formation above 10 per cent of the national income as a once-for-all effort, but keeping the economy at this high level of capital formation for at least two or three decades before it can hope to attain a self-sustaining momentum of growth. This requires a capacity not only to mobilize savings but also to "absorb" capital and invest it productively to yield a high enough rate of return to sustain the continuous process of a high rate of reinvestment, which is beyond the present capabilities of the institutional and organizational framework of many underdeveloped

* From Hla Myint, "Social Flexibility, Social Discipline and Economic Growth," *International Social Science Journal,* XVII, 2 (1964), pp. 252–259, by permission of UNESCO.

[1] W. W. Rostow, *The Stages of Economic Growth,* Cambridge, The University Press, 1960, p. 39.

countries. Similarly, condition (b) does not merely mean setting up a few factories which are indifferently run and managed and have to be maintained by heavy subsidy or protection from the government. It requires the development of the "primary growth sectors," based on innovations, new methods of production, discoveries of new resources and new ways of exploiting existing resources which will serve as the "leading sectors" to the rest of the economy. Here again the important role of the institutional framework both in stimulating these vital points of growth and in transmitting their effects to the rest of the economy is fairly obvious.

The truth of the matter is that although economic writings on the underdeveloped countries are full of proposals to launch them into self-sustained growth, only a few of these countries are ready for it. Many of them are handicapped by the lack of an effective institutional framework required for the process. To expand Professor Rostow's metaphor: a few of the underdeveloped countries, ready for the take-off, are already taxiing along the runway. For them the final spurt of speed in investment and general economic activity, if properly carried out and sustained, might conceivably enable them to become airborne. But many other underdeveloped countries have not yet got to this stage; they are still in the process of building their runways. Now, whether we are talking about aeroplanes or developing economies, we should expect the problems of getting airborne to be very different from the problems of building the runway. But unfortunately Professor Rostow does not give us very much help about the second type of problem. He has merely stated that before the underdeveloped countries are ready for the final take-off they have to pass through a long "pre-take-off" period, which in the case of the Western countries, for instance, took about a century or more. Beyond this, we are left to our own devices to try to identify the various sub-stages of the pre-take-off period at which many of the underdeveloped countries seem to be situated at the present moment, and to try to assess how far economic policies designed to assist the take-off at a later stage of development are relevant for the problems of building the runway at the earlier stages of development.

This tendency to neglect the earlier pre-take-off stages of the underdeveloped countries is of course not peculiar to Professor Rostow but is fairly widespread among economists. We have chosen his theory as our example because it is well known and also because it is explicitly stated in terms of stages of development, thus clearly revealing the gap in our knowledge about the earlier stages of economic development represented by the no-man's-land between

From the economist's side of the border, however, two distinct lines of approach have been made to explore the no-man's-land. The first consists in the various studies of the process of the spread of the money economy in the markets for commodities and for factors of production, notably labour, breaking down the self-sufficiency of the subsistence economies of the traditional societies. In this approach, the problem of stimulating economic development is looked upon mainly in terms of the growth of free market institutions and the growth of competitive economic individualism, breaking down the traditional communalism of the village, the tribe or the extended family. The general direction of development is conceived in terms of greater flexibility and adaptability of the social and economic framework, stimulating and responding to further changes. The second line of approach consists in extending the ideas of investment and capital formation originally used in relation to material capital, to "social and human capital." In this approach, the problem of economic growth is looked upon mainly in terms of increasing the rate of investment, not only in improving the physical infrastructure such as transport and communications and public utilities, but also in improving what may be called the "social infrastructure," notably in the level of education, research, technical skills and health. In order to increase the rate of investment, an increasing amount of resources has to be mobilized, and in order effectively to carry out this programme of investment both in material and human capital, the social and institutional framework must be capable of enforcing some degree of consistency and coherence both in the mobilization and in the allocation of resources. Thus the general direction of development is conceived in terms of a greater degree of social discipline and authority to push through the desired pattern of economic planning. We are faced then with the conflicting requirements of social flexibility and social discipline, a conflict which seems particulary sharp at the earlier, pre-take-off stages of development.

II

Since the broad patterns of the growth of the money economy in the underdeveloped countries are familiar, we shall concentrate on the second line of approach based on investment in social and human capital. This idea has proved attractive to many people, both economists and non-economists, and there have been attempts to consider how to strike a correct balance between investment in material capital and investment in human capital, between economic development and social development. Unfortunately, however, as currently stated this idea remains rather vague, based upon an analogy which has not been systematically drawn. Thus, as a possible subject for discussion among social scientists of different disciplines, we may begin by drawing attention to some of the conceptual problems as they appear to an economist.

To begin with, even with respect to material capital, there is no simple mechanical relationship between the amount of resources invested and the *value* of the capital formation which results from it. Although national income statistics automatically equate the two, it can readily be seen that, say, an amount of one million pounds of savings invested may result in capital goods which may be worth many times more or many times less than one million pounds, depending on how and where it is invested and how far the resultant capital goods serve the future productive requirements of the country, and how far people value the products which these capital goods can help to produce. In the extreme case, it has not been unknown that large sums of money have been so wrongly invested as to serve no useful purpose so that the value of capital formation resulting from them is zero. The problems of trying to establish a causal quantitative relation between the expenditure on resources invested and the value of capital formation which results from it are multiplied many times when we move from material capital to human capital. To start with the most general difficulty: in dealing with material capital the economists have a reasonably clear idea of what they mean by the productive structure and how an additional piece of material capital may contribute to it, either by changing and improving its efficiency or by fitting into an identifiable gap. But no such established conceptual framework exists when we move to human capital. By analogy, we must suppose that the value of a given investment in human capital will depend on its contribution to the "social infrastructure," either by improving and changing this infrastructure or by fitting into a gap in it. But what is this "social infrastructure" and in what direction do we wish to change and improve it?

At this point the economist will look askance at the social scientists from other disciplines, many of whom have been using the fashionable concept of "social and human capital" as much as some of the economists. If hard pressed to define the "social infrastructure" further, the economist can only carry the analogy one or two stages further. He would suppose that in the same way as there is an intimate connexion between the material production structure of a country and its natural resources, there would be a similar connexion between the social infrastructure and the social conditions and characteristics of a country. Material production structure represents the adaptation and improvement of natural resources through investment in material capital. Some investment would exploit the special advantages of these natural resources and other investment would make up for the deficiencies in these natural resources. He would then have to ask the other social scientists whether this analogy is meaningful when extended to cover the relationship between the social infrastructure and the social conditions of a country.

Carrying the analogy a stage further, the economist would point out that the consequences of a wrong choice of investment project may be very different between material capital and human capital. Frequently, a wrong investment in material capital and attempts to salvage it have a distorting effect on the whole production structure. For instance, a wrongly sited railway system or a factory which is a "show piece" but uneconomic may be maintained by government subsidy, grants of exclusive monopolistic privileges or protection against foreign competitors. But as a last resort a wrong investment in material capital can be scrapped when it proves too expensive to salvage. Wrong choice of investment in human capital will presumably have similar distorting effects on the social infrastructure, but wrong pieces of human capital cannot be scrapped; they tend to be self-perpetuating and have the habit not merely of distorting but actually of disrupting the social infrastructure. For instance, the growing problem of graduate unemployment in Asian countries, owing to the production of too much of the wrong type of "human capital" is a very clear illustration of this danger.[2]

In this connexion, it may be noted that for the economist the material production structure of a country is a different thing from the economic institutions which mobilize resources and feed them into the production structure. But when we come to the concept of social infrastructure, the distinction between these two different functions is blurred. As currently used, the idea of social infrastructure seems both to serve as the social equivalent of the production structure which absorbs resources and also to have the more active function of the social and institutional framework which mobilizes and allocates resources. This makes assessment of the productivity of investment in human capital doubly difficult. For instance, increased educational opportunities, say through films, radio and other mass

[2] H. Myint, "The Universities of South-East Asia and Economic Development," *Pacific Affairs,* Summer 1962.

media, may widen the horizons of the people and stimulate the growth of new wants (through demonstration effects) and new ideas. This may possibly increase the long-run productivity of the people and thus may be regarded as an improvement in the social infrastructure in the first sense. But on the other hand, the effect of these new educational opportunities may also weaken and disrupt the ability of existing social values and social hierarchies to mobilize resources and thus undermine the social infrastructure in the second sense.

III

We started by saying that the conflicting requirements of social flexibility and social discipline in promoting economic development at the earlier, pre-take-off stages of development can be illustrated by two approaches: the first in terms of the growth of the money economy, and the second in terms of increasing investment in social and human capital. It now appears that this conflict is latent even if we concentrate on the second approach only, although to some extent it is hidden by the vagueness in the concept of the "social infrastructure." Certain changes which might widen the educational horizon of a people, and thus increase their longer-run productivity, might at the same time undermine the capacity of the social and institutional framework to mobilize resources for the increase of capital formation, both human and material.

This conflict may be further illustrated by human investment in higher education for economic development where the greatest long-run increases in productivity have been frequently claimed. When people make this claim, they have two distinct ideas at the back of their minds. First, they are thinking of the dynamic effects of higher education in stimulating new discoveries and innovations and in adopting new methods of production. This implies a sort of intellectual yeast which will ferment and change the whole of the production structure and presumably the social infrastructure with it. Here the productivity of investment in human capital is conceived in terms of greater flexibility and adaptability of the social and institutional framework, which will create favourable conditions both in stimulating changes and for receptiveness and adaptability to these changes. Secondly, they are also thinking of shortages of skilled people of particular types who are needed as "missing components" to be fitted into a desired pattern of economic development. Of course, some flexibility has to be allowed even in the most rigid and comprehensive type of planning. But it is fair to say that the *basic* reasons for claiming high productivity as a result of investment in education are different in these two types of argument. In popular terms, the first type of argument is thinking in terms of creating square pegs to fit into round holes with the hope that the pattern of holes will be stretched and changed into more productive directions. The second type of argument is thinking in terms of trying to create round pegs to fit into round holes, as though fitting the missing pieces into a jigsaw puzzle within the framework of a given and fixed pattern of production and planning requirements.

These conflicting considerations become bewildering when we look closely at the skilled manpower problems of any newly independent countries. First, there is an obvious need to fill up the gaps left in the civil service, and those left in all sectors of the economy by departing foreign personnel. The missing components have to be produced to maintain the old economic and administrative structure. But at the same time there is a great desire to change very quickly "the old colonial structure," not only politically but also economically and socially. Logically, one might perhaps expect a great upsurge of a liberal educational policy encouraging individualism, enterprise and innovations to break down the rigidities both of the traditional and of the colonial systems. But given the prevailing intellectual view that such quick change can be forced through only by economic planning, the prevailing bias is against both economic liberalism and "liberal education" in favour of detailed skilled manpower planning integrated with programmes of technical education which ideally should specify the exact type of training and the exact number of trainees. Thus we get back to the problem of manufacturing the "missing components" for the jigsaw puzzle, the only trouble being that the old puzzle has been torn down and the new puzzle has not been constructed.

If the newly independent countries are vague and ambivalent about the general direction in which they wish to change their "social infrastructure," the social forces and the social and institutional framework which they can use to carry out these changes are weak and diffused and in varying stages of disintegration. On the economic side, it is well known that the growth of the money economy, while imparting flexibility, has undermined the coherence of the traditional societies. On the political side, even indirect rule through indigenous authorities has frequently had the same effect. With the new countries which have gone through an intense phase of nationalistic revolt against colonialism, this process itself has further undermined the framework of social authority and discipline. Thus the difficulties which new countries have in trying to implement their plans is not only due to the lack of technical skills and know-how, but also to a disintegration, if not a complete breakdown, of cohesive social values which contribute to social discipline.

The value of a cohesive force of social discipline in promoting economic development is now becoming increasingly recognized. The classical illustration of this is perhaps the role of the Japanese "feudal discipline" which enabled Japan's ruling classes to carry out a fairly ruthless but effective process of economic development behind a protective shell against disruptive outside influences. It would be an interesting task to find out how far the surviving traditional social institutions in a continent like Africa are capable of serving this role in promoting economic development both at the local or tribal level, such as in co-operative societies and community development schemes, and for larger units which can take advantage of the economies of scale and complementary projects. One obvious difficulty about using the traditional social forces such as "feudalism" or the caste system is the prevailing political idea of equality which raises the well known conflict between economic equality and economic growth, not only with respect to income distribution but also with respect to the distribution of economic activities and economic and social roles. To illustrate from our example of investment in education: many people, even when they stress the importance of investment in human capital, look upon the resources to be invested mainly as sums of money or material resources, such as college buildings, laboratories, libraries, hospitals, etc. But as every university teacher knows, the really scarce resource is the "human input": teachers of suitable ability and qualifications, the supply of whom cannot be expanded quickly in the short run, perhaps not dramatically even in the longer run. On the other hand, the production of further such high-quality human capital requires some restriction of entry to universities and training colleges so that those who are admitted get proper intensive training. But this conflicts with the prevailing ideals of new countries to provide university education for almost everyone, and few of the countries have been able to exercise the necessary social and political discipline to restrict numbers in this really vital process of supplying further human capital goods of suitable quality. That is to say, although most people talk about increasing "investment in education," few of them are prepared to "tighten their belts" to save the scarce teaching capacity for the training of further human capital to the minimum degree of "capital intensity" necessary to make this process a success.

THEODORE W. SCHULTZ

Investment in Man: An Economist's View*

ONCE we are of a mind that it is meaningful to examine the role that investments in man perform in an economy, a wholly new set of questions becomes relevant and important. Underdeveloped countries everywhere want to accelerate their economic growth. Most of them are strongly committed to programs of constructing new dams and power facilities, roads and harbors, factories, and above all, steel mills. Meanwhile, in many of these countries, few additional resources are being made available for training and education. The relevant and important question is clearly indicated: Are these countries making an optimum allocation of the resources at their command? To arrive at a valid answer we must use a concept of capital that includes both human and nonhuman wealth. To consider only the latter, as is almost everywhere the case, can give only misleading results. No wonder, therefore, that poor countries are in general being badly misled. There can be little doubt that they are presently allocating their resources in ways that are far from what would be required to achieve an optimum rate of growth. Harberger's study concentrated on Chile strongly supports this view, for he finds that technical advances are the key factor in achieving rapid development and that additional expenditures to improve the quality of the (technically trained) labor force are of primary importance in attaining this end.[1]

To consider a somewhat narrower question: Has India in recent years spent too much on irrigation and all too little on training her cultivators on how best to use the additional water? From reports that I get, this has been happening. The error appears to be a very costly one. In Iraq, where the government has been obtaining huge

* Reprinted from "Investment in Man: An Economist's View" by Theodore W. Schultz in *Social Science Review,* Vol. XXXIII, No. 2 (June 1959), pp. 112–17, by permission of The University of Chicago Press.

[1] Arnold C. Harberger, "Using the Resources at Hand More Effectively," to appear in the *Proceedings* of the American Economic Association (1959).

amounts of revenue from oil, the Development Board, according to Yudelman,[2] will have spent close to $1,400 million by 1960 – virtually all on flood control, irrigation, drainage, and other physical structures and only a pittance on training and education to prepare farmers and others in the use of these new facilities. Yudelman concludes that this one-sided allocation represents a most serious error in the efforts of Iraq to achieve agricultural development.

But these are the mistakes of poor countries, especially those in which there are massive governmental programs. Although we may be giving some of these countries bad economic advice, presumably this does not impair our economy. We are always ready to take comfort in our long, gradual development, in the open and decentralized character of our economy, and in our large and impressive investments in what I am calling human wealth. There is, however, no room for complacency. We, too, are constantly confronted by the same allocative problem, that is, how much or how little to invest in non-human wealth relative to what we put into ourselves. How well or how badly we are doing on this score is subject to debate. But what is not debatable is the fact that there is little or no economic analysis to draw upon because these aspects of this problem have been almost wholly neglected.

In terms of both consumption and economic growth, I have little doubt that in recent years we have been allocating altogether too many of our resources to automobiles and roads compared to what we have allocated to education. But this is an opinion; let me consider situations in which there is some evidence. Negroes on the average earn only a fraction as much as do white workers. May not much and even most of this vast discrepancy in earnings be a direct consequence of the lower productivity of Negroes arising from the deplorably bad education that they have been obtaining? Morton Zeman's study of "White and Non-White Income Differentials in the United States"[3] strongly supports an affirmative answer. The very low earnings of many of the migrant farm workers may also rest primarily on this factor.

To take still another of the serious income inequalities marked against our national record, namely, the chronic poverty of so many of the rural areas in and about the Appalachian country consisting

[2] Montague Yudelman, "Some Issues in Agricultural Development in Iraq," *Journal of Farm Economics,* Vol. XL (February 1958).

[3] Ph.D. dissertation, University of Chicago, 1958.

largely of whites: Is this poverty, also, rooted mainly in the relatively small investments that people in these areas have seen fit and have been able to make in themselves? Tang,[4] in a recent study of two groups of counties in the southern Piedmont region, has found that whereas they started from an equal income position at about the turn of the century, farm people in his "developed" counties have gained importantly in farm income per worker relative to those in his "underdeveloped" counties. This divergency in farm income per farm worker has become increasingly larger over time. Even the prosperous and full employment conditions that prevailed between 1940 and 1950 did not change this "trend toward increasing income disparity."[5] Tang's findings are not inconsistent with the industrialization hypothesis that he sought to test. A preliminary examination of his data would seem to indicate that they are also consistent with another hypothesis, namely, one based on education and related investments in people as the principal explanatory variable.

PUZZLES AND A PARADOX

Some major puzzles in our economic data may be resolved, once we take investments in man into account. As the stock of capital increases and its use deepens, we might expect the capital income ratio to increase. So it did for a long time. Kuznets[6] gives these ratios of reproducible capital to annual incomes:

Great Britain	*Ratio*
1875	4.6
1905	6.5
United States	*Ratio*
1879	2.8
1909	3.4

For the period since 1909, I return to Goldsmith.[7] His national wealth estimates also include land and, therefore, give a larger ratio than those of Kuznets, cited above. Goldsmith's ratio of national

[4] Anthony M. Tang, *Economic Development of the Southern Piedmont, 1860–1950* (Chapel Hill: University of North Carolina Press, 1958).

[5] *Ibid.*, p. 220.

[6] Simon Kuznets, "Towards a Theory of Economic Growth" (lecture at the Bicentennial Celebration of Columbia University, May 1954), Table 9.

[7] Raymond W. Goldsmith *et al.*, *A Study of Saving in the United States* (Princeton, N. J., Princeton University Press, 1956), Vol. III, Tables W-1 & N-1.

wealth to annual national income declined 25 per cent between 1909 and 1949:

Year	*National Wealth*	*Net National Income*	*Ratio*
1909	145	29	5.0
1949	898	237	3.8

[in Billions of Dollars]

If we restrict ourselves to estimates of the private sector of the United States economy, it is abundantly clear that we have not been winning our increases in income from the use of more tangible capital[8] relative to income. Between 1919 and 1957, total income rose at an annual rate of 3.1 per cent while that of tangible capital rose at a rate of only 1.8 per cent.[9] But all these estimates of capital

	Average Annual Percentage Rates of Increase			
	1889 – 1919		1919 – 1957	
1. Total output		3.9		3.1
2. Labor (weighted manhours)	2.2		0.8	
3. Capital (weighted tangible capital)	3.4		1.8	
4. Total inputs		2.6		1.0
5. Divergency: percentage line 4 is of line 1		67.0		32.0

exclude human capital represented by training, education, additional capabilities based on health and new knowledge.[10] The stock of this human capital has been increasing more rapidly than that of tangible capital; therefore, the observed decline in the capital-income ratio may be largely, or even wholly, as illusion resulting from the omission of human capital.

There is, also, the Leontief paradox indicating that the United States exports mainly wage-goods and imports largely capital-intensive goods, contrary to what one might expect for a country with much capital and with very high real wages. But here, again, no account is taken of the human capital that is represented by the acquired skills and abilities of engineers, chemists, and other workers. This human capital renders important services in the production of these wage-goods that we export. The value productivity of these particular forms of human capital may exceed that obtained on tangible (physi-

[8] As this capital is now conceived and measured.

[9] Solomon Fabricant, *Basic Facts on Productivity* (Occasional Paper No. 63 [New York: National Bureau of Economic Research, 1959]), Table 5:

[10] It is necessary to distinguish between new knowledge that becomes embedded in tangible capital and new knowledge that becomes an integral part of a people. As tangible capital is presently measured, however, even much of the new knowledge that becomes a part of it is also being missed.

cal) capital used in producing the capital-intensive goods that we import.

The central puzzle, however, the one that encompasses the others, is in our economic growth as it is revealed in the many estimates that indicate a large and increasing divergency between the rise in income and in the resources that we use to produce the additional income. Our income has been going up much the faster of the two. For example, between 1889 and 1919 the rate of increase of labor and tangible capital combined was only 67 per cent as large as that of income (both are for the private sector of the domestic economy).[11] Even so, between 1919 and 1957 the rate of increase of manhours worked and of tangible capital, taken together, was down to a mere 32 per cent of the rate at which our income rose. It is hard to believe, but wonderful if true, and if true, why? That is the puzzle.

A HUMAN WEALTH HYPOTHESIS

What is it that we have been doing that has given us a rate of economic growth that is three times as large as the rate of increase of labor and capital? My hypothesis is that the explanation is to be found in the large and rapid accumulation of human wealth that is being excluded from our conventional measures of "manhours worked" and of tangible capital.

The preliminary results from two studies lend support to this hypothesis. The first of these is based on a study that I have made of the formation of human capital, represented by education beyond the eighth grade. This form of capital not only has become very large but has been increasing much more rapidly than has the formation of conventional non-human capital.[12] In estimating the gross capital formation entailed in a high-school education, I found that in current prices it cost the U.S. economy $127 per student in 1900, and $1,493 in 1956. My estimates for college and university education are $385 for 1900 and $3,580 for 1956; most of these costs are of the nature of opportunity costs because they consist of earnings that students have foregone while they were in school studying. The national totals for all public and private schools must suffice for now; they show that only $180 million of this capital (gross) was formed

[11] See Fabricant, *op. cit.*

[12] My paper carries the title, "Gross Capital Formation Represented by High School, College, and University Education in the United States, 1900 to 1956" (AER Paper No. 5807, Department of Economics, University of Chicago, April 29, 1958).

in 1900, whereas in 1956 it had become no less than $22,700 million. To compare this increase with that of non-human capital, I need burden you with only the percentage that one was of the other in each of the two years: In 1900, the formation of this kind of capital, i.e., represented by high school, college, and university education, was only 4 per cent of that of all physical capital; by 1956 it had risen to 28 per cent of that of physical capital. This dramatic rise in the relative position of this one form of human capital, as I have measured it, nevertheless, substantially underestimates the real relative increase because I am here relying on gross capital formation figures and it is the net figures that count. There are many indications that the net figures have gone up even more because, whereas the useful life of physical capital has been declining, that of human capital has been increasing.

The other study tells us something about the rates of return on this form of human capital. Here I draw on some of the estimates that Becker[13] reported in a recent lecture. He has found that, as of 1950, males were earning a 14.8 per cent return on what they had privately invested in acquiring their high school, college, and university education, measured by their opportunity costs (earnings foregone while in school) and their direct costs (tuitions, books, etc.). When the other costs, those not borne by student or their families directly, are added to these private costs, this rate of return was still no less than 11 per cent. How does this compare with the rate of return that owners of property were obtaining? Compared to that of corporations before taxes, it is probably not very different. What about the rate of return on all non-human wealth, namely, on the approximately $1,000 billion of national wealth, as estimated by Goldsmith? This figure includes all land (agricultural, forestry, and urban), producer and consumer durables, apartment buildings and private residences, government structures, inventories, livestock, monetary metals, and net foreign assets. It is hard to believe that the 11 per cent return on this human capital did not exceed by a wide margin the rate of return that was being realized on this huge stock of non-human wealth.

It should be pointed out that in both Becker's and my study none of the private or "public" costs of this education was charged to consumption or to other important goals. This means that we have

[13] Gary S. Becker, Professor at Columbia University, in a lecture given before the Economic Development Workshop at the University of Chicago, February 5, 1959. In this lecture he drew on a major study that he has been making of the economics of education for the National Bureau of Economics Research.

overestimated the relevant costs of this kind of capital formation because a very substantial part is incurred for these other purposes and it should be attributed to them.

It should be evident that this has been a very preliminary treatment of the investments that we are making in ourselves. Education beyond the eighth grade is only one of the forms that this kind of capital formation takes, albeit a large and increasing form. Elementary education, which we take for granted, may rate even higher in what it renders to an economy. How else, for example, can one explain the early remarkable achievements in agriculture in Japan? Many poor countries are neglecting their elementary education relative to what they are spending on physical plants and equipment; moreover, the cost of this form of education is relatively low because of the low opportunity costs of taking students at that age away from other useful work.

On-the-job training is another way of accumulating some of this human capital. Still another goes back to measures that increase the strength and energy of a people and improve their health and vitality. New, useful knowledge is undoubtedly of strategic importance both in changing the nature of the useful skills that are of most value and in altering and improving the quality of the physical plant and equipment that we employ. I have not touched on the very important question of how we perpetuate this human capital in the home and through institutions other than through organized education.

I have tried to show that the state of our knowledge of investment in man is very meager. Our values and beliefs have hindered us greatly in thinking clearly about it. Economists too have missed seeing the important role that the increasing stock of human capital has come to play in the economy.

CONCLUSION

In some parts of the globe men still live in the stone age, working with stone-age implements or at times with only their bodies in an incessant struggle for survival. In other parts of the world men have come to possess and use vast quantities of highly complicated tools, machines, and structures which enable them to adapt their environment to their needs in ways unavailable even to kings in earlier times. The process of fashioning newer and better aids to production is, in essence, the process of capital formation. Conventionally, economists referred to these aids, such as machines, buildings, tools and inventories, as capital. In more recent years economists have come to stress the creation and accumulation of skills that are necessary for fashioning these tools and buildings also as capital creation (Singer). Men have to save or set aside resources (including time) from the current satisfaction of wants for investment, for the creation of tangible or intangible assets which help them produce more in the future.

But men may save or abstain from current consumption, for purposes other than investment. Economic growth necessitates that men invest their savings in productive assets such as factories rather than in monuments to gods or glory (Tangri).

Economies do not grow with capital alone—but they do not grow without it (the U.N.). Nor will saving raise productivity and standards of living significantly if it is used merely to multiply primitive (or current) tools of production. Economic development necessitates that societies be willing to encourage and accept technical and social change (Cairncross).

That more capital is desirable over time does not imply that at any given time, society should cut present consumption to the minimum so as to increase capital production to the maximum for the sake or more consumption in the future. The controversy whether capital is the key factor in or a minor contributor to the process of economic change is misplaced (the U.N. and Cairncross). It all depends on a country's particular stage of development. Some countries need institutional reforms more than capital; others are ready to absorb large quantities of capital (Galbraith). Whether capital requirements of underdeveloped countries are so large as to make their economic prospects—at least in our lifetimes—look cheerless or the requirements are more modest and savings are more plentiful than usually assumed (Myint), the underdeveloped countries will need to put in strenuous efforts to secure large amounts of investible resources.

A major part of the needed capital will have to be generated internally in each society through private or collective channels (Tangri). Usually there are large reservoirs of untapped productivity which can be utilized efficiently by a determined society to generate a growing volume of production and capital. Aid from richer countries and cooperation with other countries such as in the Alliance for Progress, can widen markets, disseminate know-how, help increase capital formation, productivity, standards of living, and the freedoms of men (Prebisch).

Considering the stake of the United States in the enlargement of human freedoms, she has given too little purely economic aid to the poor countries and needs to step up this aid significantly (Ellis).

Given certain availabilities of capital at home and abroad, should this capital be allocated to generate balanced growth or unbalanced growth? If the argument for balanced growth rests on the alleged existence of powerful vicious circles which cannot be broken otherwise, then the arguments of Hagen and Hirschman cast serious doubts on the doctrine of balanced growth. To the extent markets can be generated at home or abroad (Myint and Singer), the need for balanced growth diminishes. But if balanced growth is interpreted as the desirability of expanding supplies in relation to foreign and domestic demand (Ellis), balanced growth has a strong case.

Public authorities and planning commissions create enough imbalances without intending to. They hardly need Hirschman's encouragement to create further imbalances deliberately.

The question of proper resource allocation is still unanswered (Leibenstein). The answer depends partly on the implicit and explicit premises of economists and others concerned with development, the goals of a society and the means available to it for those goals. If population growth can be controlled or is independent of the rate of growth of income or employment and if large savings can be elicited or extracted from the population irrespective of the pattern of investment, then the neo-classical prescription of using labor-intensive techniques in capital-scarce and labor-abundant economies promises the faster route to growth in total and per capita income. But if expanded employment resulting from labor-intensive techniques leads to larger consumption and faster population growth, making further accumulation of capital and improvements in technology difficult, the solution may be with capital-intensive technology.

There is general agreement among economists as to the need for allocating capital optimally between the physical social overhead capital and directly productive activities (the U.N.), between different kinds of social infrastructure (Myint), and for optimal investment in public administration and education. Perhaps this realization is also spreading to policymakers in underdeveloped countries. The ways of determining such optimal allocations are still not very clear, but the search has begun.

Present concern with problems of economic growth and development in the underdeveloped countries is a post-World War II phenomenon. The amount of healthy controversy is characteristic of a young and sometimes undisciplined discipline. But underneath the vigorous competition and clash of ideas is a growing current of a body of commonly accepted principles and prognosis of economic development; this is especially true for the role and significance of capital accumulation as a vital, if not unique, aspect of the process of social modernization.

This growing body of knowledge, however, does not warrant much optimism about the prospects of raising living standards in the underdeveloped countries very quickly. This collection of readings has been concerned primarily with the role, requirements, uses and sources of capital formation for economic development. One negative factor, rapid population growth, has been mentioned only in passing. The application of modern medicine to medieval agricultural systems, the prevalence of welfare ideologies and the operations of private, governmental and international relief agencies are combining to bring about unprecedented rates of population growth in countries least able to support growing numbers of people. This rapid population growth, unless checked, is likely to make capital accumulation very difficult and significant gains in standards of living almost impossible to achieve, at least in this generation.

SUGGESTIONS FOR READING

A good and clear discussion of the meaning and role of capital and technology is contained in *Economic Development: Principles and Patterns*, ed. H. F. Williamson and J. H. Buttrick (New York, 1954). A strong argument against forcing the pace of development through capital accumulation or otherwise is offered by S. Herbert Frankel's *The Economic Impact on Underdeveloped Societies* (Oxford, 1953). Works emphasizing the noneconomic factors in economic growth include Everett E. Hagen, *The Process of Social Change* (Homewood, Illinois, 1962); Bert F. Hoselitz, *Sociological Aspects of Economic Growth* (New York, 1960); *Development and Society: The Dynamics of Economic Change*, ed. Joseph A. Schumpeter, David E. Novack and Robert Lekachman (New York, 1964); and David C. McClelland, *The Achieving Society* (Princeton, 1961).

Ragnar Nurkse's pioneering book, *Problems of Capital Formation in Underdeveloped Countries* (Oxford, 1953), and W. Arthur Lewis' eclectic work, *The Theory of Economic Growth* (London, 1955), are easy and rewarding reading. Joan Robinson's *The Accumulation of Capital* (Homewood, Ill., 1956), is for sturdier souls.

For a more extended treatment of the concept of the big push, P. N. Rosenstein-Rodan's classic article, "Problems of Industrialization of Eastern and South-Eastern Europe," *Economic Journal* (June–September 1943), should be supplemented by his "Notes on the Theory of the 'Big Push'" in *Economic Development for Latin America*, ed. Howard S. Ellis (New York, 1961), and "Programming in Theory and in Italian Practice," in *Investment Criteria and Economic Growth*, published by the Center for International Studies, Massachusetts Institute of Technology, Cambridge, 1955. A rigorous development of a related concept is to be found in Harvey Leibenstein, *Economic Backwardness and Economic Growth* (New York, 1957). A scholarly Marxist point of view is presented in Paul A. Baran, *The Political Economy of Growth* (New York, 1957), while the case for free markets and against excessive governmental regulation and control is presented forcefully by Jacob Viner in *International Trade and Economic Development* (New York, 1952), and Harry G. Johnson, *Money, Trade and Economic Growth* (London, 1962). Two short and clear expositions of the role of international trade are Ragnar Nurkse, *Patterns of Trade and Development* (New York,

1961), and Gerald M. Meier, *International Trade and Development* (New York, 1963).

The best discussions of resource allocation criteria presume a good command of economic theory; sample readings would include: Otto Eckstein, "Investment Criteria for Economic Development and the Theory of Welfare Economics," *Quarterly Journal of Economics*, Vol. LXXI, No. 1 (Feb. 1957), pp. 56–85; R. S. Eckaus, "The Factor Proportions Problem in Underdeveloped Areas," *American Economic Review*, Vol. XLV, No. 4 (Sept. 1955), pp. 539–65, and Hollis B. Chenery, "Comparative Advantage and Development Policy," *American Economic Review* (March 1961), pp. 18–51; A. K. Sen, *Choice of Techniques* (Oxford, 1962); S. Chakravarty, *The Logic of Investment Planning* (Amsterdam, 1959); and J. Tinbergen, *The Design of Development* (Baltimore, 1958).

An excellent collection on balanced vs. unbalanced growth (and on several other issues) is in *Leading Issues in Economic Development*, ed. Gerald M. Meier (New York, 1964). For discussions on planning a useful reference is *Planning Economic Development*, ed. Everett E. Hagen (Homewood, Illinois, 1963).

Gary S. Becker, "Investment in Human Capital: A Theoretical Approach," Selma J. Mushkin, "Health as an Investment," and the contributions of the October 1962 supplement of *The Journal of Political Economy* are of interest to students of social infrastructure.

M. F. Millikan and W. W. Rostow make a case for foreign aid in *A Proposal: Key to an Effective Foreign Policy* (New York, 1957), while a case against aid is presented in Milton Friedman, "Foreign Economic Aid: Means and Objectives," *Yale Review* (June 1958). *Why Foreign Aid?*, ed. Robert A. Goldwin (Chicago, 1963), contains a variety of viewpoints.

1234567890